One Pot: Three Ways

Rachel Ama

One Pot: Three Ways

Save time with vibrant, versatile vegan recipes

Rachel Ama

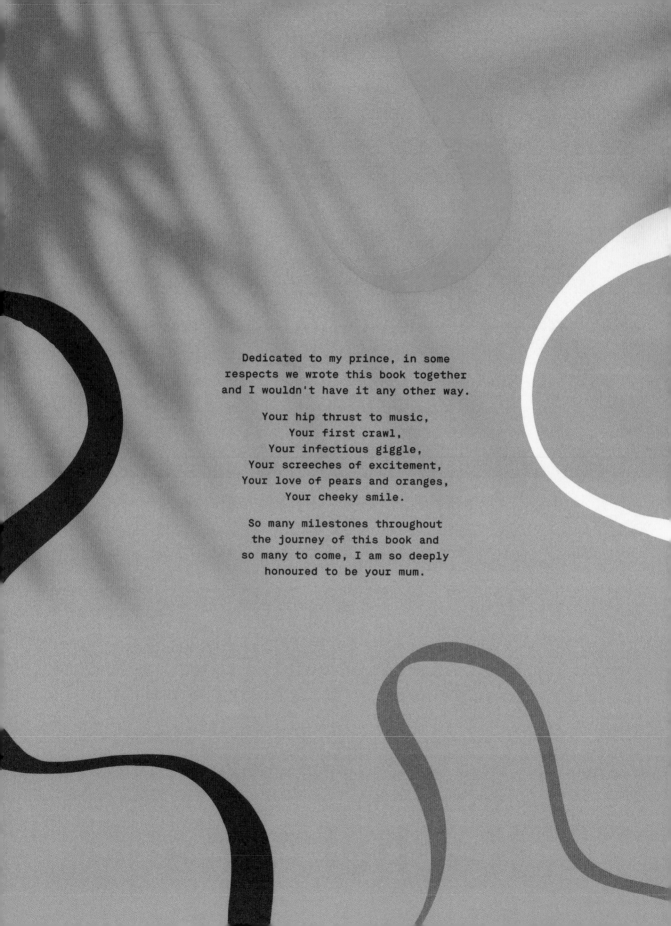

Dedicated to my prince, in some
respects we wrote this book together
and I wouldn't have it any other way.

Your hip thrust to music,
Your first crawl,
Your infectious giggle,
Your screeches of excitement,
Your love of pears and oranges,
Your cheeky smile.

So many milestones throughout
the journey of this book and
so many to come, I am so deeply
honoured to be your mum.

CONTENTS

Rachel
Ama

Wholesome, Flavourful, Plant-based

About six years ago, I made the decision to switch to a vegan diet, and since then I've found an entirely new excitement, love and enjoyment in the food I create, eat and share. As someone who absolutely loves delicious food, I can honestly say that I've never enjoyed food as much as I have on this plant-based journey. Wholesome, flavourful food that makes you feel good is worth celebrating. Nothing beats sitting down with a delicious meal and taking the time to enjoy it – it's one of life's many gifts. Imagine a summer's day, a kitchen full of simple, seasonal fruits and vegetables, with the windows and backdoor open, the smell of aromatics cooking in the pan, and, of course, one of my playlists in the background – that is my happy place. And this book lets me share my happy place with you.

Becoming vegan

It's strange to think that this vegan way of eating was once completely new to me, but it took me a while to get here.

It started with dairy. Dairy – especially cheese – seems to be a big factor for people when they're considering going vegan, with many wondering how they could live without it. The truth is that dairy and I have always had a pretty turbulent relationship. I'd had unresolved health problems for years, but at the time none of the health professionals I spoke to had made any kind of link between my health issues and my diet. My mum has always been a firm believer that what we eat affects our bodies, so she encouraged me to practise a 'process of elimination', cutting out different foods and keeping a record of how it affected my health. I quickly identified dairy as the culprit – it was causing inflammation throughout my body, resulting in various knock-on effects. Those problems faded within months, and disappeared after a year, so I always big up my mum for her guidance. I think one of the last times I ate dairy was from a famous pizzeria in Boston. I will never forget that oh-so-cheesy pizza – but nor will I forget how it left me feeling! (Awful... for weeks.) Cheese is a vice for many people, but it's an enemy to my progress and my system – something I believe is true for almost everyone in varying degrees. Back then, it was hard to find non-dairy alternatives, but today there's an AMAZING range!

While I'd removed dairy from my diet, I was still eating meat or fish most days. Growing up in a city, I had never really been exposed to farming practices and the journey food takes on its way to our kitchens – I just saw the packaged product. But after learning more about how food ended up on my plate, I knew, ethically, that I could no longer be a part of that process. So almost overnight, I decided to stop eating animal products. That was it.

In addition to my ethical reasons for going vegan, I also wanted a change for myself. As I'd already experienced health benefits from removing dairy from my diet, cutting out all animal products felt instinctive to me. I wanted to centre my love for food in fruits, vegetables and nutritious whole foods. I wanted my body to thrive. And that's exactly what happened. Through

many happy hours experimenting in my kitchen – and with the help and support of the amazing and enthusiastic following I've engaged with online – I've developed a way of cooking and eating plant-based foods that indulges my love of flavour and makes me feel great. My food is a reflection of the different influences and experiences I've had, the people I've met and the tables I've sat at. I love finding new flavours, rediscovering old favourites and exploring ways to create plant-based versions of dishes I've always loved.

I've been lucky enough to do a fair amount of travelling. Some of my adventures have taken me road tripping across the States, travelling across different countries in South America, I've spent British winters in the Caribbean, as well as taken trips to Europe and Indonesia. I've enjoyed incredible food that keeps me so inspired when cooking at home. As well as growing up in London, full of different cultures and cuisines, my heritage plays a huge role in the food I make: my immediate family are Welsh, St Lucian and Sierra Leonean, so it's fair to say I grew up visiting family members with very different-smelling kitchens across London, and each smells like home to me. In saying that, it's no secret that Caribbean food is my favourite; the flavours and aromas are very close to my heart and always put a big smile on my face.

Finding a new star of the show

I love sharing my recipes, whether that's online, in books or in person. I've been lucky enough to cook and give food demonstrations at festivals and other large food events, which give me the chance to share my big, plant-based flavours with as many people as possible. Seeing other people enjoy my food gives me so much energy. To my continuing joy, people really engage with these demos and always want to learn more. At the end of each show, demonstration or interview, I am always hit with the same question: 'How do you eat vegan every day?' It's a great question, and it's one of the reasons I'm so excited to be sharing this book. Because there is a secret to it – and it can unlock a whole new way of cooking and eating.

Whether you go completely vegan or just decide to start eating more plant-based meals, a lot of people – including me – have to kind of re-learn how to cook. Most of us, especially in the UK, grow up with the understanding that our meals should centre around meat or fish, served with a carb and a vegetable on the side. Most of our daily meals are put together using this basic formula, and often that fish or meat centrepiece will be rolled out in various guises over the next few days as the leftovers are used up. In my house, for example, we'd typically have a big roast chicken on a Sunday, then the leftover meat would form the basis of our meals for the next couple of days.

When I decided to go vegan, those centre-pieces I was so used to cooking suddenly weren't there any more, which left me with an entire meal made up of what I'd previously considered to be 'sides'. That prospect can leave you thinking,

'Erm... how can that be filling?'... Or even nice to eat? But as I began to get more comfortable with my new, plant-based way of eating, I unconsciously began cooking in the same way. I didn't realise it at first, but I'd begin with a big pot or tray of something delicious, then roll it out over the next few days, either serving it the same way each time, or changing things up with different variations to create a whole new dish. It varied, depending on how creative I was feeling, or how much time I had to spend in the kitchen making dinner. Instead of meat or fish, though, my new 'centrepiece' would be some kind of delicious vegetable or legume. For me, this approach made sticking to my new vegan diet a lot easier, and helped me find new ways to cook plant-based foods that were both delicious and filling. (Plus, of course, it's a great way of eating more sustainably and avoiding food waste – win-win.)

And that's what we're going to do in this book. Make a big pot, pan or tray full of food on a Sunday (or any day you like), then roll it out over the next day or so in different, fun and delicious ways – making a fresh new feast with yesterday's leftovers!

I've found that this way of cooking takes away the pressure of 'Ugh, what am I gonna make for dinner?', or that feeling of not having enough time to put together a feast from scratch. Your tasty centrepiece is there, ready and waiting in the fridge or freezer. This book will set it all out for you, with three exciting and tasty ways to use each centrepiece recipe, helping plant-based eating feel more achievable (and delicious).

How to Use This Book

To make things super simple, I've developed each of the easy but bold and flavourful centrepiece recipes using either **ONE POT**, **ONE PAN** or **ONE TRAY** to serve 4. Then you can choose from three different ways to transform your centrepiece into a gorgeous meal.

For example, on Sunday, you might make **Cajun Beer-battered Oyster Mushrooms** (page 102) in one tray and serve it that night with **Garlicky Crushed New Potatoes**; on Monday, you can transform it into **American-style 'Chicken' Pickle Sandwich**; and on Tuesday, you can create **Cajun Tacos with Pickled Red Onion & Tartare Sauce**. Alternatively, if you find the serving style on Monday was so delicious that you want to eat exactly the same meal the next night, be my guest – the choice is yours.

Servings

Each centrepiece recipe makes 4 servings so it's really easy to scale up or down. Just double it up to make 8 servings if you want to do some big batch cooking.

Each centrepiece recipe comes with three ways of serving it, and each way serves 2 – simply double it up to serve 4.

Main Recipe

Cajun Beer-battered Oyster Mushrooms

(serves 4)

Option One

Garlicky Crushed New Potatoes

(serves 2)

Option Two

American-style 'Chicken' Pickle Sandwich

(serves 2)

Option Three

Cajun Tacos with Pickled Red Onion & Tartare Sauce

(serves 2)

Different Ways to Use the Recipes

1

2

One-off Recipe for 4 people

Perfect for when you're having friends over or you just want to create a big family meal, but you don't really want or need leftovers.

Make 1 centrepiece recipe. Choose your preferred 'way' recipe and double it up to serve 4.

Meals for 3 Days for 2 people

Great for when there's just a couple of you and you want to plan out some meals.

Scale up a centrepiece recipe by 1.5 to create 6 servings. Each day, choose 1 of the 3 'way' recipes to serve it.

3

~~~

Meals for 3 Days for 4 people

Perfect for feeding a family for 3 days.

Scale up a centrepiece recipe by 3 to create 12 servings. Each day, choose 1 of the 3 'way' recipes and double it up to make 4 servings.

4

~~~

Feast Days

For when you really want to go all out and have a full-on feast for yourself and/or your friends and family. Check out the feasting images in each chapter for inspiration (see pages 42–3, 120–1 and 136–7).

Scale up your chosen centrepiece recipe by 1.5 to make 6 servings. Make 1 of each of the 3 'way' recipes (giving you 6 servings in total) and let everyone dive in.

My heritage plays a huge role in the food I make; my immediate family are Welsh, St Lucian and Sierra Leonean, so it's fair to say I grew up visiting family members with very different-smelling kitchens across London, and each smells like home to me.

Rachel Ama

My happy place

My Kitchen Rules

OK, so these days, my kitchen has new rules. Here's a bit of a breakdown.

There are **three main stations**. First up is the fridge and fresh corner, where all the fresh ingredients hang out – all the things that don't last too long. In the fridge, there are ingredients like kale, spinach, peppers and salad, but there are also a few fresh ingredients that don't live in the fridge, like potatoes and onions. Next there's the 'pantry' (if you're feeling fancy – store cupboard if you're not!), which is where all the legumes and grains live – things like rice, quinoa, chia seeds, chickpeas and black beans – as well as cans of tomatoes, coconut milk and passata. Basically your canned or dried goods. Third – and perhaps most important – is the flavour station. This is where you'll find all the spices, such as cumin, turmeric and allspice, dried herbs and those all-important sauces and condiments that really bring things to life, such as rice vinegar, hot sauce and harissa paste.

We keep stations two and three pretty well-stocked, as these items have relatively long shelf lives, so we only need to top them up every month or so when items run out. The fridge, however, is where we focus on the fresh produce and being as sustainable as we can, which means not buying excess. With this book, you'll often find that the 'way' recipes simply require mixing in a few different fresh ingredients. You might just need to pick up something like tomatoes, cucumber and fresh parsley on your way home from work, and you'll have the makings of a new feast using yesterday's leftovers.

What I love about making big pots of vegetable stews and curries is that you can add leftover vegetables to them at any time. If you've got half an onion sitting sadly in the bottom of the fridge, or a forgotten chunk of courgette in need of a new home, you can just pop them into the pot when you're transforming your centrepiece into whatever feast you're going to enjoy that day. Have fun with it, and use up what you've got!

Over the next few pages I've listed the key ingredients and foods I like to have on hand in my different kitchen stations. As mentioned above, I tend to keep stations two and three well-stocked, while station one gets restocked more regularly. I like to plan out my meals for the next few days so I know what fresh ingredients I need to pick up.

Fridge & Fresh Top-up Essentials

tomatoes // onions // garlic // cucumber
spinach // beetroot // avocados // peppers
mushrooms // aubergines // courgettes
sweet potatoes // potatoes // squash // kale

Store-cupboard Essentials

rice (white, brown, mixed) // chickpeas
quinoa // pasta (penne, spaghetti, fusilli)
butterbeans // lentils (French, Puy, red)
black beans // coconut milk // passata

Sauces & Flavour-station Essentials

I've gone into a little more detail here so you can get really familiar with all these amazing oils, condiments, herbs and spices. This is where the magic happens, and these incredible flavour boosters will brighten up any leftovers. A few of these flavour-station superstars overleaf actually live in the fridge when they're not busy taking your cooking to the next level, but you'll see why they belong in this category.

Flavour-station essentials to brighten up any leftovers

~

Tahini

Once you find your favourite tahini brand, I guarantee an addiction will take over! Made with ground sesame seeds, tahini is creamy, slightly nutty, savoury and flavourful, with a rich, full-bodied mouthfeel perfect for topping vegetables, adding to salad dressings, or, for some people, serving with anything. You can even use tahini in sweet treats, such as cakes, because of its richness. A simple tahini dressing needs no more than a kick of acidity, a little sweetness, salt and occasionally a touch of water to loosen it (depending on the brand).

Dried red chilli flakes

When you want to control the fiery heat in a particular dish, chilli flakes are your friend. They are especially useful if you are cooking for multiple people with different spice tolerances, as those who like it hot can scatter over extra before digging in.

Lemon & lime

A kick of natural acidity to brighten up different foods. A splash of lemon or lime juice can bring full flavours to life, creating a sense of freshness and refreshing your palate. Of course, all types of citrus juice are great for salad dressings, but a dash of lemon added right at the end of cooking will transform your food. Seasoning is not simply salt and pepper, but acidity and salt. Fun fact: a nice amount of acidity can reduce the amount of salt needed to make your dishes flavourful. You can also try a splash of red wine vinegar in rich sauces.

Miso paste

Miso is said to have originated in China, where Buddhist priests experimented with fermenting salts, soya beans and grains as a way of preserving food. However, miso paste is also associated with Buddhist priests in Japan, where it is valued for its health benefits, intense savoury taste and ability to preserve food. Its umami richness adds a depth of flavour similar to cooking with meats. Typically made with fermented soya beans, miso paste is nowadays made with other fermented legumes, such as chickpeas, which are similarly effective in heightening flavour. It is seriously delicious and perfect for richly flavoured stews, pasta sauces and soups.

Harissa paste

An incredibly delicious hot chilli paste that originated in Tunisia, although variants of it can be found all across North Africa. I would love to list a bunch of different versions, but I always find rose harissa the most accessible and delicious. You can find it at most supermarkets and it's an easy way of adding a good kick of flavour in a short amount of time. It's perfect for stews and amazing for using as a glaze on grilled vegetables.

Fresh herbs

Enjoyed in every cuisine, fresh herbs always take food to another level. I love them on pretty much every meal! If I had to be specific for someone new to cooking with fresh herbs, I would recommend parsley (specifically the curly leaf variety) with all my Italian-inspired meals, coriander on anything Caribbean or Latin-inspired, and mint on fresh salads and in Middle Eastern-inspired dishes. However, don't limit a herb to any one cuisine, as they can be enjoyed across the board! Don't be shy with them. Start exploring, find your favourite and brighten up your plate.

Extra-virgin olive oil, peanut oil, sesame oil, etc

Here is some info for oil lovers. Take any rich pasta dish, and just before serving, drizzle an organic extra-virgin olive oil on top. The mouthfeel and flavour of the dish is immediately elevated. You're not cooking the oil – you are enjoying its natural flavour and texture. The same can be done with a bowl of hot sesame soba noodles: drizzle a touch of good-quality sesame oil on top just before serving and, again, notice the difference. This doesn't work unless the oils are really good quality – preferably cold-pressed, organic and extra-virgin.

Rice vinegar, balsamic vinegar, white wine vinegar, red wine vinegar

Used for both cooking and baking, vinegars help to balance salt and fat in food, and thereby improve flavours. They also make vegan cakes fluffy and can preserve food. Having vinegar(s) on the shelf is therefore really important.

Vegetable stock

A flavoursome liquid base made by simmering vegetables and different aromatic ingredients in water. There are a lot of ready-made vegan-friendly vegetable stocks in today's world, and they can add a quick burst of flavour to your food. My current go-to stocks are based on wild mushrooms, as these pack a good punch of flavour.

Spices & spice blends

Keep a good range, such as sweet paprika, cumin, garlic powder, allspice, turmeric, madras curry powder, nutmeg and cinnamon.

Dried herbs

I find the most useful dried herbs are parsley, oregano, thyme, rosemary, sage, bay leaves and curry leaves.

Vegan cooking hacks

Whether you're new to vegan cooking or just want to take your plant-based creations up a notch, these easy vegan hacks will take your food to the next level.

Miso paste

As well as using it in traditional Far Eastern recipes, I also love adding miso paste to recipes usually based on meat, such as bolognese sauce, rich stews and hearty pies. It has an almost unique ability to add a salty, savoury flavour – another layer of complexity that boosts almost any dish. There are different types of miso, ranging in colour from light to dark, and also varying slightly in taste. My current go-to for 'cheezy' sauces is white miso paste, while for rich stews I favour brown rice miso paste.

Cornflour: concentrate those flavours & thicken things up

A staple when it comes to thickening sauces, marinades, gravies, pie fillings, desserts and glazes. I find cornflour most helpful when making sauces, as it never goes lumpy. You can begin by layering up the flavours with different spices and aromatics, and add umami notes with miso paste, soy sauce, nutritional yeast or even mushrooms. The final touch is then to thicken up the sauce and concentrate those flavours by adding a simple cornflour slurry. Never add cornflour straight into hot liquids – always start by mixing one part cornflour with one part water. Whisk to combine, and you have your slurry. Pour this into your hot liquid and stir to thicken. (Common substitutes: Arrowroot, rice flour, tapioca starch, potato starch.)

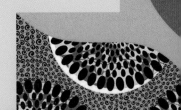

Mushrooms: the unbeatable natural vegan texture king

There once was a time when I detested mushrooms, and quite a few friends of mine felt the same until I showed them different types of mushrooms and cooking techniques that allow them to carry flavours and showcase their amazing textures. Oyster mushrooms are my favourite, hands down. You can roast them, grill them, deep-fry them in batter... however you prepare them, they truly are incredible. They are succulent, tender and slightly chewy, and hold flavour so well that I've tricked a few of my mushroom-hating friends into loving them. Usually the response is: 'Huh? How is this a mushroom?' For the full chargrilled experience, barbecue some oyster mushrooms and coat them in barbecue jerk sauce or regular barbecue sauce – I promise you won't feel like you're missing out on meat. Being mild in flavour, mushrooms are great for dousing in your favourite flavours, whether spicy, smokey, sweet or herby. Or deep-fry them in a crispy, flavourful batter, like my Cajun Oyster Mushrooms on page 102 – proof that mushrooms rock!

Salt, acid, fat: bring out the best in your food

There is an entire book on the subject of flavour and texture in cooking because they are so important. Salt brings out the flavours in food, and I particularly like cooking with Maldon sea salt flakes or Himalayan salt. Fat helps to make delicious textures, but also amplifies flavours. Among my favourites are extra- virgin olive oil, coconut oil, sesame oil, coconut milk, cashew nuts and peanut butter. Acid adds a brightness that helps to balance the food, I very often use lime in this book, but my other favourites are lemon, apple cider vinegar, red wine vinegar, rice vinegar and white wine vinegar. Building a balance is key to intensifying the flavours on your plate. Feel free to start experimenting in the kitchen, trying to balance your favourite combos to bring out the best in all your cooking experiments.

Fresh herbs: lift your plate with fresh flavourful herbs

The most common and accessible fresh herbs are usually coriander, parsley, dill, chives, basil, mint, sage, thyme and rosemary. Whether grown on a windowsill or in a garden, or bought from a shop, they are an affordable and delicious way to brighten up your plate. My everyday go-to is curly leaf parsley. I dash it over stews, pasta, potatoes, roast veggies – so many things! I recommend tasting lots of different herbs to find your favourite. Just a handful can completely refresh and revitalize a plate of leftovers. As herbs can lose their aroma over time, I love to sprinkle them on top of a dish just before I'm about to eat it. I also use them to add a delicate aroma to a big pot of food, or to create a marinade with oil, garlic and fresh chillies. If you are new to herbs, you can start small and relatively safe with the herbs listed above, then spread your wings and try out the wonderful flavours of, say, marjoram, lovage or tarragon.

Griddle pan: quick caramelization and juicy flavours

If you don't have a barbecue (perhaps because you don't have space, or you live somewhere where 'barbecue weather' is not a common occurrence), a griddle pan is your next best bet. There is something extremely delicious about grilled vegetables, from aubergines and courgettes to mushrooms and peppers. With a griddle pan, you can achieve really quick and easy caramelization on your veggies while retaining texture – no sogginess here! Just add any of your favourite flavours or spice mixes for really quick, tasty results.

Vegemite or yeast extract

Salty, tangy, and pungent, yeast extract does a similar umami job as miso paste, but is soy-free. Stir a spoonful of it into your vegetable shepherd's pie, vegan chilli, rich brothy soups and marinades for an elevated level of flavour.

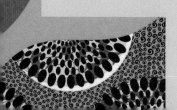

3 Key Kitchen Tools for Mastering Your Centrepiece

~~

 **One pot**

I love to have a good, deep casserole dish that is oven-safe and has a lid for locking in flavours. This is probably my most-used type of pot, whether I'm making stews, curries or pasta. Choose one that can be placed in the oven for long, slow cooking, not just on the hob.

 **One pan**

Everyone needs a large, reliable frying pan, preferably at least 24cm (9½in) in diameter, perfect for pan-frying chickpeas, sautéing vegetables and even making stir-fries. My preferred type of pan is one that has a bit of depth so that I can also use it like a wok for stir-frying (perfect if, like me, you don't actually have a wok, or your wok has had its day). I also use my frying pan for shallow-frying things, such as plantain, beer-battered vegetables, homemade chips and fritters.

One tray

A good, large roasting tray is essential for me. How else am I going to cook all those gorgeous, fluffy but crispy roast potatoes? Chucking a bunch of leftover vegetables in a roasting tray is one of the quickest, easiest ways to use up whatever you've got. Sometimes I coat them in something spicy – perhaps garam masala, harissa or jerk seasoning, and sometimes in fresh herbs, lemon and garlic – so simple and fuss-free. For extra protein, chickpeas and butter beans both roast really well, as you'll see on pages 146 and 152. My preferred roasting tray is one that can go on the hob as well as in the oven. This can be handy if you want to toast your spices before roasting your food – not essential, but definitely handy. I love versatile cookware. Choose a roasting tray with sides that have a little bit of height, perfect for when you're making something with a sauce, or just have big potatoes to roast.

One
Pot

<u>Chapter One</u>

Caribbean Jackfruit Brown Stew

Makes 4 servings

1 tbsp vegetable oil

1 red onion, finely chopped

2 spring onions, finely chopped

1 red pepper, finely sliced

1 green pepper, finely sliced

3 garlic cloves, finely chopped

thumb-sized piece of fresh root ginger, finely chopped

1 tsp sweet smoked paprika

1 tsp allspice

1 tbsp browning

200g (7oz) cooked black beans, drained

4 large tomatoes, roughly chopped

2 x 400g (14oz) cans young jackfruit in water, drained and rinsed

500ml (18fl oz) vegetable or mushroom stock

½ Scotch bonnet chilli, seeded

1 tbsp maple syrup

1 tsp liquid smoke (if you can't find this, use soy sauce)

1 tbsp brown rice miso paste

4 fresh thyme sprigs

1 tbsp cornflour

/ You can omit the browning, but this is why the dish has the name 'brown stew'.

Inspired by 'brown stew chicken', a staple dish in almost every Caribbean household. I've kept all those memorable flavours and spices here and cooked it slowly so the jackfruit tenderizes and locks in the umami richness with a touch of spice and sweetness. I also love to make this from dried black beans if I have time.

If you're fancying something fun, serve up my **Brown Stew Cheezy Tacos [1]** – dip them back into the stew to get them extra saucy. For a super-quick hearty meal, stir through some soft **Fusilli [2]**. Alternatively, serve it up my favourite way, with **Rice & Peas, Plantain & Tahini Apple Cabbage Slaw [3]**.

Heat the oil in a large pot or saucepan over a medium heat. Add the red onion, spring onions and red and green peppers, and cook for 3 minutes until beginning to soften. Then add the garlic, ginger, paprika, allspice and browning and cook, stirring, for a further 2 minutes. If the mixture starts to stick to the saucepan, add a little more vegetable oil or a small splash of water to loosen.

Stir in the black beans, tomatoes, jackfruit and stock, then add the Scotch bonnet, maple syrup, liquid smoke and brown rice miso paste. Give the stew a good stir, then add the thyme and cover. Reduce the heat to low and leave to cook for 1 hour, stirring occasionally, until the jackfruit has become tender and loose enough to roughly break down with a spoon.

In a small jug or bowl, mix the cornflour with 2 tablespoons water to form a slurry. Stir this into the stew and allow to cook for another 5 minutes, uncovered, until slightly thickened.

The stew is now ready to be used in the recipes on pages 26–8, or it will keep in the fridge for 3 days, or in the freezer for 3 months.

Brown Stew Cheezy Tacos

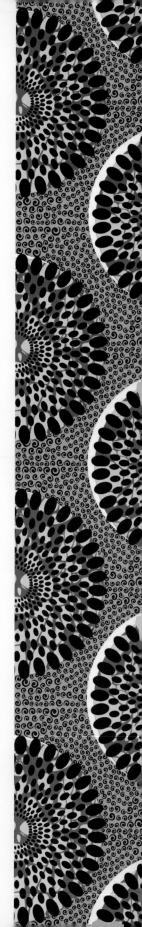

Option
One

Serves 2

~~~

2 portions of Caribbean Jackfruit Brown Stew (page 24)

1 tbsp vegetable oil

6 small tortillas

6 slices vegan cheese

TO SERVE

handful of fresh coriander, chopped

1 onion, finely sliced

2 limes, cut into wedges

6 tsp hot sauce

1 avocado, peeled, stoned and sliced

Heat the stew in a saucepan over a low heat for 10 minutes until piping hot.

Meanwhile, heat the oil in a frying pan. Add 1 tortilla and toast for 1 minute until slightly crisp. Turn over and place a slice of vegan cheese on top of the tortilla, followed by a large spoonful of hot jackfruit stew. Fold over the tortilla to make a semicircle. Cover the pan with a lid and cook for a few minutes to help melt the vegan cheese, before turning to cook the other side. Transfer to a warm plate and repeat this process with the remaining tortillas.

Serve the tacos sprinkled with coriander and onion slices, and arrange the lime wedges, hot sauce and avocado on the side. Place any remaining stew in a bowl for dipping.

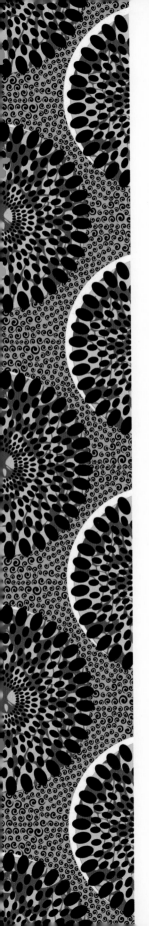

Jackfruit Brown Stew Fusilli

Option Two

Serves 2

~

200g (7oz) fusilli

2 portions of Caribbean Jackfruit Brown Stew (page 24)

sea salt and freshly ground black pepper

TO SERVE

handful of fresh flat-leaf parsley, roughly chopped

2 tbsp macadamia nuts, crushed

2 tbsp nutritional yeast (optional)

2 tsp extra-virgin olive oil

Cook the pasta according to the packet instructions in a large pot of salted boiling water until al dente. Before draining, set aside a cup of the pasta water and reserve, then drain as normal.

Place the jackfruit stew in a large, deep saucepan over a medium heat to warm through. Once hot, add the cooked pasta and stir to combine. Add some of the reserved pasta water, a spoonful at a time, to help loosen the sauce slightly. I usually use 3 large spoonfuls.

To serve, season with black pepper, sprinkle over the parsley, macadamia nuts and nutritional yeast, if using, and drizzle over the extra-virgin olive oil.

Rice & Peas, Plantain & Tahini Apple Cabbage Slaw

/ Option Three

Serves 2

~~

2 portions of Caribbean Jackfruit Brown Stew (page 24)

2 tbsp olive oil

1 ripe plantain, peeled and cut into 2cm (1in) slices

TAHINI DRESSING

2 tbsp tahini

1 tsp maple syrup

1 tbsp extra-virgin olive oil

1 tbsp lime

½ tsp lime zest

sea salt and freshly ground black pepper

SLAW

¼ white cabbage, shredded

1 apple, cored and sliced into matchsticks

1 carrot, grated

1 spring onion, finely chopped

handful of fresh flat-leaf parsley, roughly chopped

RICE & PEAS

2 garlic cloves, finely sliced

1 spring onion, finely sliced

1 tbsp olive oil

200g (7oz) basmati rice, rinsed well under running water

½ x 400g (14oz) can red kidney beans

240ml (8¼fl oz) coconut milk

2 fresh thyme sprigs

sea salt and freshly ground black pepper

Begin by making the tahini dressing. Place all the ingredients in a small bowl or jug with 1 tablespoon water and mix well to combine. Different types of tahini can vary in thickness, so if the dressing is too thick, add another splash of water to loosen.

For the slaw, place the cabbage, apple, carrot, spring onion and parsley in a large bowl. Pour over the dressing and mix to combine. Set aside to allow the cabbage to absorb the dressing while you prepare the rest of the dish.

To prepare the rice and peas, sauté the garlic and spring onion with the oil in a frying pan over a medium heat for 4 minutes until they begin to soften.

Add the rice, followed by the kidney beans, coconut milk and 200ml (7fl oz) water. Season with salt and black pepper to taste and stir in the thyme. Bring to the boil, then cover and reduce the heat to low. Simmer for 10 minutes until all the liquid has been absorbed. Remove the lid and fluff the rice with a fork.

Meanwhile, for the plantain, heat the oil in a frying pan over a medium heat. Add the plantain slices in a single layer and cook for 5 minutes until golden brown, then flip to cook on the other side. Once cooked, place on a piece of kitchen paper to remove excess oil. Season with a sprinkle of sea salt before serving.

To reheat the Caribbean Jackfruit Brown Stew, place in a deep saucepan over a medium heat. Add a splash of water, bring to the boil, then reduce the heat and simmer with the lid on for 6 minutes, stirring occasionally, until piping hot.

Harissa Hotpot

Main Recipe

Makes 4 servings

1 tbsp olive oil

1 tbsp rose harissa paste

1 tsp sweet smoked paprika

½ tsp ground cinnamon

2 red onions, finely sliced

thumb-sized piece of fresh root ginger, minced

2 aubergines, quartered lengthways, then chopped into triangular slices

1 x 400g (14oz) can chickpeas, drained

2 x 400g (14oz) cans tomatoes

zest and juice of ½ orange

sea salt and freshly ground black pepper

GARNISH

handful of fresh flat-leaf parsley

2 tbsp shelled pistachio nuts, crushed

In this hotpot, aubergines and chickpeas are flavoured with aromatic ginger, cinnamon and fragrant harissa and all cooked in one big pot in the oven. This is a simple way to intensify flavours quickly and achieve very happy kitchen smells. The aubergines become deliciously soft and absorb all the flavours.

Serve the hotpot with **Wild Rice [1]** flecked with kale and tossed in infused oil and lemon juice, topped with fresh parsley and crunchy pistachio nuts. For a speedy lunch, serve warm with **Toasted Garlic Sourdough with Rocket [2]** – the garlic parsley rub is too good! For a warming salad, serve it alongside my **Green Tahini & Green Bean Salad [3]** – it's simply crunchy lettuce and salted green beans with a tahini dressing that has a herby hit.

Preheat the oven to 200°C/180°C fan/400°F/gas 6.

Heat the olive oil in a deep, ovenproof pot over a medium heat. Add the harissa paste, paprika, cinnamon and onions and cook for 5 minutes until the onions are translucent. If they begin to stick to the pan, add a splash of water to loosen them. Add the ginger and aubergines and mix to combine, then stir in the chickpeas, tomatoes and orange zest and juice. Season with salt and black pepper.

Cover the pot with a lid and place in the oven. Cook for 20 minutes, then remove from the oven and stir. Return to the oven for another 20 minutes until the aubergines have softened.

Garnish with the fresh parsley and pistachio nuts before serving with your choice of option dish.

The hotpot is now ready to be used in the recipes on pages 32–3, or it will keep in the fridge for 3 days, or in the freezer for up to 3 months.

Garlic, Lemon & Kale Wild Rice

Option One

Serves 2

125g (4½oz) wild rice, washed under cold running water

2 portions of Harissa Hotpot (page 30)

2 tbsp extra-virgin olive oil

2 garlic cloves, minced

handful of kale, roughly chopped and any woody stalks removed

1 tbsp lemon juice

sea salt and freshly ground black pepper

handful of fresh flat-leaf parsley, to garnish

1 avocado, peeled, stoned and sliced, to serve

Place the rice in a large saucepan with 250ml (9fl oz) water. Season with salt and stir. Place over a high heat and bring to the boil, then cover, reduce the heat to low and simmer for 45 minutes, or until all the liquid has been absorbed.

Meanwhile, warm the hotpot in a deep saucepan over a high heat. Bring to the boil, then reduce to a low heat and simmer for 6 minutes, stirring occasionally, until piping hot.

Heat the oil in a saucepan or frying pan over a low heat. Add the garlic and cook gently for 5 minutes, taking care not to burn it. Add the kale and cooked wild rice. Increase the heat to medium and stir together for 3 minutes until the kale is slightly wilted. Finally, squeeze in the lemon juice and season with salt and black pepper.

Serve the rice with the hotpot, garnished with fresh parsley, and with sliced avocado on the side.

Toasted Garlic Sourdough with Rocket

Option Two

Serves 2

2 portions of Harissa Hotpot (page 30)

4 tbsp olive oil

2 garlic cloves, minced

1 tbsp freshly chopped flat-leaf parsley

4 thick slices of sourdough bread

handful of fresh rocket

sea salt and freshly ground black pepper

lemon wedges, to serve

Preheat the oven to 220°C/200°C fan/425°F/gas 7.

Warm the hotpot in a deep saucepan over a high heat. Bring to the boil, then reduce to a low heat and simmer for 6 minutes, stirring occasionally, until piping hot.

Meanwhile, place the olive oil, garlic and parsley in a small bowl, mix together and season with sea salt and black pepper.

Brush a generous amount of the mixture on both sides of each slice of bread. Place the bread on a baking tray and bake in the oven for 10 minutes, turning halfway through. Remove from the oven and serve the toasted garlic sourdough alongside the harissa hotpot, with fresh rocket on the side and lemon wedges for squeezing over.

Green Tahini & Green Bean Salad

Option
Three

Serves 2

2 portions of Harissa Hotpot (page 30)

300g (10½oz) green beans, trimmed

1 Little Gem lettuce, leaves separated

1 tbsp extra-virgin olive oil

GREEN TAHINI DRESSING

¼ tsp ground cumin

½–1 tsp maple syrup

handful of fresh flat-leaf parsley, finely chopped

handful of fresh coriander, finely chopped

2½ tbsp tahini

2 garlic cloves, grated

1 tbsp fresh lemon juice

sea salt

Warm the hotpot in a deep saucepan over a high heat. Bring to the boil, then reduce to a low heat and simmer for 6 minutes, stirring occasionally, until piping hot.

Meanwhile, make the dressing. Place all the ingredients for it in a bowl, adding just ½ teaspoon maple syrup at first. Add 2 tablespoons water and mix well until smooth. Some tahini brands can be thicker or more bitter than others, so taste the dressing: if it is too bitter, add a little more maple syrup; if it is too thick, add an extra splash of water to loosen. Set aside.

Fill a saucepan with salted water and bring to the boil. Add the beans and boil for 2–3 minutes until tender, but still rich in colour and with a slight bite. Drain well, then place in a large salad bowl. Add the lettuce leaves, then drizzle over the dressing and the extra-virgin olive oil. Toss the salad together and season to taste with salt before serving alongside the hotpot.

This bean salad can be eaten warm or at room temperature.

Caribbean Curried Jack

Makes 4 servings

2 tbsp vegetable oil

1 tsp ground turmeric

1 tsp allspice

2 tbsp Madras curry powder

1 tbsp tomato purée

2 x 400g (14oz) cans young jackfruit in water, drained and rinsed

1 x 400g (14oz) can black eyed beans, rinsed and drained

500ml (18fl oz) vegetable stock

¼ tsp freshly ground black pepper

1 tbsp soy sauce

4 fresh thyme sprigs

2 large tomatoes, chopped

1 large potato, chopped into 1cm (½in) chunks

2 carrots, chopped into 1cm (½in) chunks

½ Scotch bonnet chilli, seeded and finely chopped

CURRY PASTE

1 onion, roughly chopped

thumb-sized piece of fresh root ginger

4 garlic cloves

2 spring onions

My favourite thing about going to a cookout, barbecue or wedding with my Caribbean friends and family was knowing I'd be tucking into some curried mutton or goat. Since becoming vegan, I wanted to enjoy that dish but in a plant-based way. Jackfruit is the hero for adding texture and absorbing all the aromatic curry spices for that authentic reminder of one of my favourite meals. It's especially good when cooking your very own cookout – check out pages 42–3. You can also swap the jackfruit for your favourite vegan meat substitute.

The first option is to serve this curry with **Coconut Rice & Coleslaw [1]** – pure comfort! Refresh the leftovers with some incredibly simple-to-make, warm and soft **Coconut Flatbreads with Tomato & Red Onion Salad [2]**. Tear off a piece and dip it into your hot, fragrant curry, or wrap the curry inside, as you would in a roti, and serve alongside the onion and tomato salad mixed with fragrant herbs. Alternatively, turn the curry into flaky, buttery, hot and spicy **Caribbean Patties with Orange & Avocado Salad [3]**, which are much easier to make than most people think. With the fresh salad, this to me is what summer dreams are made of.

Place all the curry paste ingredients in a food processor and blend to form a coarse paste. Heat the oil in a large saucepan over a medium heat. Add the curry paste, followed by the turmeric, allspice, curry powder and tomato purée. Stir to combine, then reduce the heat to low and cook for 5 minutes.

Now add all the remaining ingredients. Increase the heat to high and bring to the boil, then reduce the heat to a low simmer, cover and cook for 20 minutes. Now that the jackfruit has softened start to squash and separate it with the back of a spoon so it becomes stringy - it will look like pulled chicken. Remove the lid, stir, and cook for another 10 minutes until the potato and carrots have softened.

The curry is now ready to be used in the recipes on pages 36–40, or it will keep in the fridge for 3–5 days, or in the freezer for up to 3 months.

Coconut Rice & Coleslaw

Option
One

Serves 2

2 portions of Caribbean Curried Jack (page 34)

handful of fresh coriander, freshly chopped

COCONUT RICE

200g (7oz) basmati rice

240ml (8¼fl oz) coconut milk

COLESLAW

1 carrot, grated

¼ white cabbage, shredded

3 tbsp vegan mayonnaise

sea salt and freshly ground black pepper

SALAD

2 plum tomatoes chopped

1 Little Gem lettuce, leaves torn

1 avocado, peeled, stoned and sliced

1 tbsp extra-virgin olive oil

juice of 1 lime

Place the rice in a large saucepan along with the coconut milk and 200ml (7fl oz) water. Season with salt and stir. Bring to a gentle simmer over a medium heat, then cover, reduce the heat to low and cook for 10 minutes, or until all the liquid has been absorbed. Remove the lid and fluff the rice with a fork.

Meanwhile, warm the curry in a saucepan over a high heat. Bring to the boil, then reduce the heat to a simmer for 6 minutes until the curry is piping hot. If it is too thick, a splash of water will loosen it a little.

To make the coleslaw, mix the carrot and cabbage together in a large bowl. Tip in the vegan mayonnaise, season to taste with salt and pepper and mix to create a creamy slaw.

In a separate large bowl, toss all the salad ingredients together.

Serve the hot curry in a bowl alongside the coconut rice and salad, topping it with fresh coriander.

Coconut Flatbreads with Tomato & Red Onion Salad

Option Two

Serves 2

2 portions of Caribbean Curried Jack (page 34)

lime wedges, to serve

TOMATO & RED ONION SALAD

4 large tomatoes, sliced

1 large red onion, sliced

2 tbsp extra-virgin olive oil

1 tbsp balsamic vinegar

handful of fresh coriander, roughly chopped

sea salt and freshly ground black pepper

COCONUT FLATBREADS

200g (7oz) unsweetened coconut yoghurt

200g (7oz) self-raising flour, plus extra for dusting

¼ tsp ground cumin

¼ tsp ground coriander

½ tsp baking powder

½ tsp salt

To make the salad, mix the tomatoes and red onion together in a large bowl. Drizzle over the olive oil and vinegar. Season to taste with salt and pepper, and top with some of the fresh coriander. Set aside until needed.

Meanwhile, warm the curry in a saucepan over a high heat. Bring to the boil, then reduce the heat to a simmer for 6 minutes until piping hot. If the curry is too thick, a splash of water will loosen it a little.

Place all the flatbread ingredients in a large bowl and mix together to form a dough. On a lightly floured surface, knead the dough for 1 minute until smooth, adding a little extra flour if it is too wet. Divide the dough into 4 equal pieces and flatten each one with a rolling pin or your hand to a thickness of about 2cm (1in).

Heat a non-stick frying pan over a high heat until hot, then add the flatbreads in batches. Cook for 30 seconds on each side until lightly browned.

Serve the curry alongside the hot flatbreads and red onion salad, with a wedge of lime on the side. Sprinkle with the remaining fresh coriander before serving.

Caribbean Patties with Orange & Avocado Salad

Option Three

Serves 2

2 portions of Caribbean Curried Jack (page 34)

170g (6oz) plain flour, plus extra for dusting

1 tsp ground turmeric

1 tsp salt

1 tsp curry powder

100g (3½oz) coconut oil (in its solid state)

1 tsp white vinegar

4–6 tbsp ice-cold water

1 tbsp olive oil

1 tbsp maple syrup

1 tbsp extra-virgin olive oil

1 tbsp fresh lime juice

grated zest of 1 orange

2 ripe avocados, peeled, stoned and sliced

2 ripe oranges or blood oranges, peeled and sliced into 1cm (½in) chunks

1 carrot, sliced into ribbons

70g (2½oz) rocket

½ red onion, finely sliced

handful of fresh coriander

sea salt and freshly ground black pepper

Start by making the patties. Place the flour, turmeric, salt and curry powder in a blender and quickly pulse to combine. Add the coconut oil and pulse until the mixture resembles breadcrumbs. Add the vinegar and 4 tablespoons of the ice-cold water and pulse again. It should start to come together.

Transfer the mixture to a lightly floured surface and knead to form a dough. If it seems too dry, add a little more water. Set aside in the fridge for 20 minutes.

Preheat the oven to 200°C/180°C fan/400°F/gas 6 and line a baking tray with baking paper.

Divide the chilled dough into 4 equal pieces and roll each into a circle about 13cm (5in) in diameter and 4mm (¼in) thick. Place a large spoonful of the cold curry in the centre of each circle, then fold over the pastry to create a semicircle. Using a fork, crimp the edges to seal.

In a small jug or bowl, mix together the olive oil and maple syrup, then gently brush this mixture over the top of the patties. Place on the prepared tray and bake for 20 minutes until lightly golden.

Meanwhile, make the salad. Mix the olive oil, lime juice and orange zest together in a small bowl or jug.

Arrange the avocado, orange slices, carrot, rocket and onion on a serving plate or in a salad bowl. Drizzle over the dressing, season with salt and pepper and top with fresh coriander. Set aside until needed.

Remove the patties from the oven and leave to cool for 5 minutes before eating.

Lemongrass Coconut Curry

Main
Recipe

Makes 4 servings

1 tbsp coconut oil

2 carrots, peeled and sliced

½ butternut squash, peeled, seeded and cut into 2.5cm (1in) cubes

1 x 400ml (14fl oz) can coconut milk

2 tbsp soy sauce

100g (3½oz) baby corn

100g (3½oz) mangetout

sea salt

CURRY PASTE

thumb-sized piece of fresh root ginger

2 lemongrass stalks, trimmed and tough outer layers removed

4 garlic cloves

2 red chillies

1 red onion, roughly chopped

handful of fresh coriander and stalks

1 tbsp mild curry powder

Whip up this delicious curry paste infused with citrusy and slightly tart lemongrass, then cook in rich coconut milk with vibrant veggies. It makes a bright and fragrant curry.

Simply serve it up with some **White Rice & Fresh Coriander [1]** as a speedy dinner. Roll over the leftovers by roasting a butternut squash and turning this curry into a simple **Lemongrass & Butternut Squash Soup [2]**, and serve topped with a generous spoonful of creamy coconut yoghurt. You can also use the base to make a light and comforting fragrant broth, transforming it into **Lemongrass & Vermicelli Noodle Soup [3]** with tender edamame beans, topped with a sprinkling of chilli flakes and a squeeze of fresh lime juice.

To make the curry paste, place all the ingredients for it in a food processor and blend to form a coarse paste.

Heat the oil in a large pot over a medium heat. Add the curry paste and stir-fry for about 4 minutes, until fragrant, reducing the heat if necessary to prevent browning. Add the carrots and butternut squash, mix well, then stir in the coconut milk and soy sauce, along with 80ml (2¾fl oz) water. If the liquid doesn't quite cover the vegetables, add a little more water. Season with salt and stir again. Bring to a gentle simmer, then cook for 20 minutes, stirring occasionally, until the butternut squash has softened.

Add the baby corn and mangetout and cook for another 4 minutes.

The curry is now ready to be used in the recipes on pages 46–9, or it will keep in the fridge for 3 days, or in the freezer for up to 3 months.

White Rice & Fresh Coriander

Option One

Serves 2

~~~

2 portions of Lemongrass Coconut Curry (page 44)

200g (7oz) basmati rice, rinsed under cold running water

TO SERVE

1 spring onion, sliced

1 tbsp chilli flakes

handful of fresh coriander

sea salt

lime wedges

Warm the curry in a saucepan over a high heat. Bring to the boil, then reduce the heat to low and simmer for 6 minutes, stirring occasionally, until piping hot. If it begins to thicken, add a splash of water.

Meanwhile, place the rice in a deep saucepan over a high heat and cover with 480ml (16fl oz) water. Season with salt and bring to the boil, then reduce the heat to low. Cover and leave to cook for 10 minutes, or until all the water has been absorbed. Remove from the heat and fluff up the rice with a fork.

Sprinkle the rice with the spring onion, chilli flakes and fresh coriander, and serve with the curry, offering lime wedges on the side for squeezing.

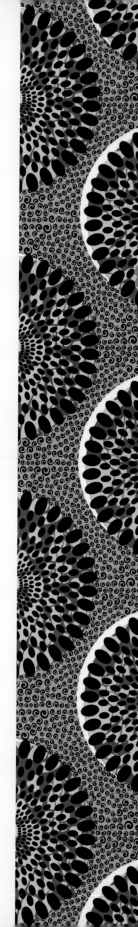

Lemongrass & Butternut Squash Soup

Option
Two

Serves 2

½ butternut squash, seeded

2 tsp extra-virgin olive oil

2 portions of Lemongrass Coconut Curry (page 44)

90ml (6 tbsp) vegetable stock (optional)

2 tbsp unsweetened coconut yoghurt

1 tbsp chilli flakes

sea salt and freshly ground black pepper

1 lime wedge, halved

handful of fresh coriander, chopped

Preheat the oven to 210°C/190°C fan/410°F/gas.

Place the butternut squash, cut-side up, on a roasting tray. Drizzle with the olive oil and season to taste with salt and pepper. Roast for 40 minutes until soft and tender.

Add the cooked butternut squash to a blender along with the curry. Blend until smooth. Pour the mixture into a deep saucepan and warm through over a medium heat until piping hot. If the soup seems too thick, add the vegetable stock to loosen it.

To serve, divide between two bowls, stir in the coconut yoghurt, then scatter over the chilli flakes and fresh coriander. Squeeze the juice of a lime wedge over, then season with black pepper.

Lemongrass & Vermicelli Noodle Soup

Option
Three

Serves 2

300g (10½oz) vermicelli rice noodles

2 tsp white miso paste

2 portions of Lemongrass Coconut Curry (page 44)

1 tbsp soy sauce

150g (5½oz) edamame beans, podded

TO SERVE

1 spring onion, chopped

1 tbsp chilli flakes

handful of fresh coriander, roughly chopped

lime wedges

Fill a deep saucepan with boiling water, then add the vermicelli noodles and cook for 10 minutes (or according to the packet instructions) until al dente. Before draining, reserve 320ml (10¾fl oz) of the cooking water and set aside, then drain the noodles as normal. Set the noodles aside until needed.

In a small jug, mix together the reserved noodle water and the white miso paste.

Place a clean, deep saucepan over a medium heat and add the lemongrass curry. Add the white miso mixture and the soy sauce and stir to combine. Bring to the boil over a high heat, then reduce to a low simmer and cook for 6 minutes. Add the edamame beans and cook for another 2 minutes until piping hot.

To serve, divide the noodles between 2 bowls and cover with the lemongrass curry soup. Garnish with the spring onion, chilli flakes and coriander, offering lime wedges on the side for squeezing over.

Heart of Palm Moqueca

Makes 4 servings

1 tbsp coconut oil

1 red onion, finely diced

1 red pepper, sliced

1 green pepper, sliced

2 tsp sweet smoked paprika

1 tbsp chilli flakes

1 tbsp tomato purée

4 garlic cloves, minced

1 x 400ml (14fl oz) can coconut milk

200ml (7fl oz) vegetable stock

1 x 400g (14oz) can hearts of palm, sliced lengthways, then chopped into 2.5cm (1in) diagonal chunks

300g (10½oz) cherry tomatoes, halved

1 tbsp capers

juice of 2 limes

20g (¾oz) fresh flat-leaf parsley

20g (¾oz) fresh coriander

sea salt and freshly ground black pepper

This Bahia-style moqueca (seafood stew) reminds me of the month I spent travelling around Brazil. The traditional Brazilian moqueca is made with coconut milk, tomatoes, fresh herbs and a good hit of lime or lemon. This vegan-friendly version uses heart of palm, a delicious vegetable harvested from the centre of cabbage palm trees. It has a tender yet firm texture that lends itself incredibly well to this citrusy, salty and refreshing stew that takes me right back to Brazil. If you can't get hold of palm hearts, the recipe also works with jackfruit, white beans or your favourite meat substitute.

Serve it with some **Butter Beans, Garlic Sourdough & Green Beans [1]** and use that crusty warm bread to dip into all those Bahia-style juices. Refresh it later by heating it through to serve with **Herby New Potatoes [2]** and a handful of peppery, crisp watercress. Then simply transform the leftovers into a super-indulgent, rich **Creamy Pasta [3]** with green peas and cheesy nutritional yeast.

Heat the coconut oil in a large saucepan over a medium heat. Add the onion and red and green peppers and fry for 5 minutes. Stir in the paprika, chilli flakes, tomato purée and garlic and cook for another 2 minutes.

Pour in the coconut milk and vegetable stock, followed by the hearts of palm, cherry tomatoes and capers. Season with a pinch of sea salt and black pepper. Bring to a simmer, then reduce the heat to low and cook for 30 minutes until the tomatoes have softened completely. Add half the lime juice, then taste, and if like me you love a good kick of lime, add the rest. Cook for another 5 minutes. Turn off the heat and sprinkle in the parsley and coriander.

The moqueca is now ready to be used in the recipes on pages 52–3, or it will keep in the fridge for 3 days, or in the freezer for up to 3 months.

Butter Beans, Garlic Sourdough & Green Beans

Option One

Serves 2

2 portions of Heart of Palm Moqueca (page 50)

1 x400g (14oz) can butter beans, drained and rinsed

4 tbsp olive oil

2 garlic cloves, minced

4 thick slices of sourdough bread

200g (7oz) green beans, trimmed

1 tsp extra-virgin olive oil

sea salt

handful of fresh parsley, chopped

Place the moqueca and butter beans in a deep saucepan over a medium heat and cook until piping hot.

Meanwhile, combine the olive oil, salt and garlic in a small bowl. Brush a generous amount of this mixture on both sides of each slice of bread. Place the bread on a baking tray and bake in the oven for 10 minutes, turning halfway through.

Bring a saucepan of salted water to the boil. Once boiling, add the green beans and cook for 2–3 minutes until tender but still rich in colour and with a slight bite. Drain well. Place the beans in a bowl and season with salt, then drizzle over the olive oil.

Serve your moqueca and butter bean mixture in a bowl alongside the garlic sourdough, and top with the green beans and fresh parsley.

Herby New Potatoes

Option Two

Serves 2

500g (1lb 2oz) new potatoes, chopped so they are evenly sized

2 portions of Heart of Palm Moqueca (page 50)

2 tbsp extra-virgin olive oil or vegan butter

handful of fresh flat-leaf parsley, roughly chopped

handful of fresh chives, roughly snipped

sea salt and freshly ground pepper

TO SERVE

1 red chilli, seeded and finely sliced

handful of watercress

1 avocado, peeled, stoned and sliced

Place the potatoes in a large pot and cover with water. Season with salt, then place over a high heat and bring to the boil. Once boiling, reduce the heat to medium and simmer for 10 minutes until the potatoes are easily pierced with a fork.

Meanwhile, place the moqueca in a saucepan over a high heat and bring to the boil. Reduce the heat to low and simmer for 6 minutes, stirring occasionally, until piping hot. If it begins to thicken, add a splash of water.

Drain the potatoes, then return them to the pan, pop the lid on and give the pan a shake to break them up. Drizzle over the olive oil and sprinkle with the parsley and chives. Season with salt and pepper. Serve with the chilli, watercress and avocado.

Moqueca Creamy Pasta

Option Three

Serves 2

50g (1¾oz) cashew nuts, soaked for at least 1 hour

2 garlic cloves

4 tbsp nutritional yeast

150g (5½oz) frozen green peas

250g (9oz) penne pasta

2 portions of Heart of Palm Moqueca (page 50)

handful of fresh flat-leaf parsley, roughly chopped

sea salt and freshly ground black pepper

Drain the soaked cashew nuts and place in a high-speed blender. Add 120ml (4fl oz) water along with the garlic and nutritional yeast. Season with salt and pepper and blend until completely smooth.

Cook the peas in a small saucepan of boiling water for 3 minutes, then drain and set aside.

Cook the pasta in a large pot of boiling water seasoned with salt until al dente. When ready, reserve a cup of the cooking water, then drain the pasta as normal. Return the pasta to the pot, place over a medium heat and pour in the cashew nut sauce. Add the moqueca and cooked peas, and stir to combine. Cook for 3–5 minutes until piping hot, mix in the peas, then add a splash of the reserved pasta water. Season with salt and pepper and serve garnished with fresh parsley.

Date & Chickpea Tagine

Main
Recipe

Makes 4 servings

1 tsp olive oil

2 red onions, grated

3 garlic cloves, finely chopped

thumb-sized piece of fresh root ginger, grated

1 tsp ground cumin

2 tsp paprika

½ tsp ground cinnamon

½ tsp ground coriander

½ tsp cayenne pepper

1 tbsp tomato purée

1 aubergine, chopped into 2.5cm (1in) cubes

1 carrot, chopped into 1cm (½in) half-moons

300g (10½oz) sweet potatoes, peeled and chopped into 1cm (½in) cubes

2 x 400g (14oz) cans tomatoes

1 x 400g (14oz) can chickpeas, rinsed and drained

300ml (10fl oz) vegetable stock

90g (3¼oz) dates, stoned and roughly chopped

4 small preserved lemons, cut into thin strips

pinch of saffron

fresh flat-leaf parsley, to serve

A tagine is a slow-cooked North African stew traditionally made in an earthenware clay pot called a tagine, hence its name. My vegan version allows you to sample the beautiful aromatic spices and flavours of that dish in your home kitchen, using a deep casserole pot. The recipe is sweetened with luxurious dates, which melt into the sauce, while preserved lemons sharpen it with a citrus tang.

Remix this pot of warming flavours into **Vegan Meatballs & Brown Rice [1]** and serve with a coconut mint yoghurt for a hearty weekday meal. Or pair with **Toasted Almond & Mint Couscous [2]** topped with colourful pomegranate seeds. To carry through those North African flavours, serve it with **Lemon-roasted Potatoes & Chermoula [3]**.

Heat the oil in a large, ovenproof pot over a medium heat. Add the onions, garlic and ginger and cook for 5 minutes, stirring often. Add the ground spices and tomato purée and cook for a further 5 minutes until the onions are tender. If the spices start to stick to the bottom of the pot, splash in a little water or oil to loosen.

Stir in the aubergine, carrot and sweet potatoes, followed by the tomatoes, chickpeas and stock. Finally, add the dates, preserved lemons and saffron. Stir, bring to the boil and season with salt. Cover the pot, transfer to the oven and cook for 30 minutes.

Remove from the oven and stir. If the sweet potatoes have not yet softened, return to the oven for another 10 minutes.

When the tagine is ready, sprinkle with fresh parsley before serving. It is now ready to be used in the recipes on pages 56–60, or it will keep in the fridge for 3 days, or in the freezer for up to 3 months.

Vegan Meatballs & Brown Rice

Option
One

Serves 2

~~~~

200g (7oz) brown rice, rinsed well under cold running water

1 tbsp olive oil

200g (7oz) vegan meatballs

2 portions of Date & Chickpea Tagine (page 54)

handful of fresh flat-leaf parsley

1 tsp chilli flakes

sea salt

MINT YOGHURT

50g (1¾oz) coconut yoghurt

1 tbsp fresh lemon juice

1 tsp extra-virgin olive oil

handful of fresh mint, chopped

handful of fresh coriander, chopped

Place the rice in a deep saucepan over a high heat and cover with 500ml (18fl oz) water. Season with salt and bring to the boil, then reduce the heat to low, cover with a lid and leave to cook for 45 minutes, or until all the water has been absorbed. Remove from the heat and fluff up the rice with a fork.

For the mint yoghurt, place all the ingredients in a bowl and stir to combine.

While the rice is cooking, heat the oil in a saucepan over a medium heat. Add the vegan meatballs and cook according to the packet instructions until golden brown all over. Add the tagine to the pan and mix well. Cook for a further 5–7 minutes, stirring occasionally, until piping hot.

To serve, divide the rice and meatballs between two bowls with a large spoonful of the mint yoghurt, and scatter over the fresh parsley and chilli flakes.

Toasted Almond & Mint Couscous

Option Two

Serves 2

~~~

2 portions of Date & Chickpea Tagine (page 54)

100ml (3½fl oz) water or vegetable stock

2 tsp extra-virgin olive oil

100g (3½oz) couscous

¼ cucumber, finely sliced

juice and zest of ½ lemon

2 tbsp sliced toasted almonds

handful of fresh mint

30g (1oz) pomegranate seeds

sea salt and freshly ground black pepper

Warm the tagine in a saucepan over a high heat. Bring to the boil, then reduce to a low heat and simmer for 6 minutes, stirring occasionally, until piping hot. If it begins to thicken, add a splash of water.

Meanwhile, place a saucepan over a high heat and add the stock or water, plus 1 teaspoon of the oil. Bring to the boil, then stir in couscous. Cover with a lid, remove from heat and leave to steam for 5 minutes. Fluff up with a fork.

Combine the sliced cucumber, lemon juice and zest in a bowl and stir in the remaining oil. Season with salt and pepper.

Sprinkle the toasted almonds, mint and pomegranate seeds over the couscous, then serve with the tagine and the cucumber salad.

Lemon-roasted Potatoes & Chermoula

Option Three

Serves 2

2 portions of Date & Chickpea Tagine (see page 54)

LEMON-ROASTED POTATOES

2 medium potatoes, peeled and cut into wedges

1 tbsp olive oil

2 tbsp fresh lemon juice (see Tip)

2 garlic cloves, smashed

120ml (4fl oz) vegetable stock

CHERMOULA

1 preserved lemon, flesh and pith scraped away

100g (3½oz) fresh coriander

30g (1oz) fresh flat-leaf parsley

2 garlic cloves

¼ tsp ground cumin

¼ tsp sweet paprika

2 tbsp extra-virgin olive oil

sea salt

/ For extra lemony potatoes, pop the lemon wedge in the roasting tray too.

Preheat the oven to 220°C/200°C fan/425°F/gas 7.

Place the potatoes in a single layer in a roasting tray. Drizzle over the olive oil and lemon juice, then add the garlic and vegetable stock. Roughly mix together and place in the oven. Roast for 20 minutes, then give it all a good stir and roast for another 30 minutes until golden brown.

Meanwhile, to make the chermoula, place all the ingredients in a food processor and pulse into a loose paste. You can also make this with a pestle and mortar by roughly chopping the ingredients and then pounding them into a loose paste.

Warm the tagine in a saucepan over a high heat. Bring to the boil, then reduce the heat to low and simmer for 6 minutes, stirring occasionally, until piping hot. If it begins to thicken, add a splash of water.

Serve the potatoes and chermoula alongside the tagine.

Tomato & Butter Bean Minestrone

Main
Recipe

Makes 4 servings

1 tbsp olive oil

1 onion, grated

1 leek, finely sliced

2 carrots, grated

4 garlic cloves, minced

1 tbsp sundried tomato paste
or regular tomato purée

3 x 400g (14oz) cans tomatoes

600ml (20fl oz) vegetable stock

2 x 400g (14oz) cans butter beans,
drained and rinsed

1 tbsp chilli flakes

1 tsp dried oregano

1 tbsp brown rice miso paste

2 large handfuls of kale, roughly
chopped and any woody stalks
removed

sea salt and freshly ground black
pepper

This hearty tomato-based Italian soup includes butter beans, carrots, leeks, salty sundried tomatoes and a generous amount of kale, which all make it really satisfying. Minestrone was traditionally made in order to use up leftover vegetables and beans, so if you have any of those things needing to be cooked, feel free to add them. The recipe is a great way of clearing out your fridge! This simple minestrone is extremely comforting, nourishing and delicious – perfect for family dinners.

To make **Pasta e Fagioli [1]**, another favourite Italian soup, add some cooked conchigliette pasta shells or ditalini – always a crowd-pleaser in my house. Switch it up next by thickening the soup and serving it with fluffy on the inside/crispy on the outside **Baked Potatoes & Vegan Sausages [2]**. For a more substantial dinner, serve with **Courgettes, Yellow Peppers & Brown Rice [3]**. Spoon that luscious sauce over the rice to bring out all those flavours.

Heat the oil in a large, deep saucepan over a medium heat. Add the onion, leek and carrots, season with salt and pepper and cook for 10 minutes, stirring occasionally.

Add the garlic and sundried tomato paste and fry for a further minute, then add the canned tomatoes, vegetable stock, butter beans, chilli flakes and oregano. Stir in the miso paste and bring to the boil, then reduce the heat to low and cover. Leave to simmer, stirring occasionally, for 20 minutes, then remove the lid and cook uncovered for another 10 minutes. Turn off the heat and add the kale, stirring until it has wilted. Season to taste with salt and pepper.

The minestrone is now ready to be used in the recipes on pages 64–5, or it will keep in the fridge for 3 days, or in the freezer for 3 months.

Pasta e Fagioli Soup

Option
One

Serves 2

150g (5½oz) conchigliette pasta shells or ditalini

2 portions of Tomato & Butter Bean Minestrone (page 62)

sea salt

TO SERVE

1 tbsp extra-virgin olive oil

2 tbsp nutritional yeast

1 tbsp chilli flakes

handful of fresh flat-leaf parsley, roughly chopped

Cook the pasta in a large pot of salted boiling water according to the packet instructions until al dente. When ready, reserve a cupful of the cooking water, then drain the pasta and return it to the pan. Add the minestrone and the cupful of pasta water and bring to the boil over a high heat. Reduce to low and simmer for 6 minutes until warmed through. Add the cooked pasta and simmer for another minute.

To serve, divide the mixture between 2 bowls. Drizzle over the extra-virgin olive oil, then sprinkle with the nutritional yeast, chilli flakes and parsley.

Baked Potatoes & Vegan Sausages

Option
Two

Serves 2

2 baking potatoes

4 vegan sausages

2 portions of Tomato & Butter Bean Minestrone (page 62)

2 tbsp vegan butter

handful of fresh flat-leaf parsley, roughly chopped

sea salt and freshly ground black pepper

Preheat the oven to 220°C/200°C fan/400°F/gas 7.

Prick the potatoes several times with a fork. Place them directly on the oven shelf and bake for 1 hour, or until crisp on the outside and soft inside.

Meanwhile, cook the sausages according to the packet instructions until golden brown.

Warm the minestrone in a saucepan over a high heat. Bring to the boil, then reduce the heat to low and simmer for 6 minutes, stirring occasionally and allowing the sauce to reduce slightly, until piping hot.

Cut the baked potatoes in half and add a dollop of vegan butter to each one. Season with salt and pepper. Top with the minestrone mixture, sprinkle over some fresh parsley and serve with the sausages.

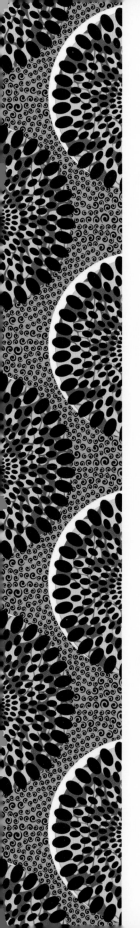

Courgettes, Yellow Peppers & Brown Rice

Option
Three

Serves 2

200g (7oz) brown rice, rinsed well under cold running water

1 tsp olive oil

1 courgette, chopped into 2.5cm (1in) diagonal slices

1 yellow pepper, chopped into 2.5cm (1in) cubes

2 portions of Tomato & Butter Bean Minestrone (page 62)

handful of fresh coriander

1 tsp chilli flakes

sea salt and freshly ground black pepper

lemon wedges, to serve

Place the rice in a pot over a high heat and cover with 500ml (18fl oz) salted water. Bring to the boil, then reduce the heat, cover and leave to cook for 45 minutes or until all the water has been absorbed.

Meanwhile, place the oil in a saucepan over a medium heat. Add the courgette and yellow pepper, and season with a generous pinch of salt and pepper. Cook for a few minutes until the courgettes and peppers have lightly browned, then turn over and cook for another few minutes to lightly brown the other side.

Place the minestrone in a separate pot over a high heat for 6 minutes, stirring occasionally, until piping hot.

Serve the minestrone mixture over the cooked brown rice, top with the courgettes and peppers, and sprinkle with the coriander and chilli. Offer the lemon wedges on the side, for squeezing over.

Winter Stew

Makes 4 servings

1 tbsp olive oil

3 carrots, peeled and sliced diagonally into 1cm (½in) slices

4 shallots, peeled and halved

300g (10½oz) oyster mushrooms (or use shiitake mushrooms)

2 bay leaves

6 fresh thyme sprigs

2 tbsp plain flour

250ml (9fl oz) red wine

1 x 400g (14oz) can plum tomatoes

150g (5½oz) sweet potatoes, peeled and roughly cubed

500ml (18fl oz) vegetable stock

1 tbsp brown rice miso paste

sea salt and freshly ground black pepper

handful of fresh curly leaf parsley, roughly chopped, to serve

Nothing quite beats a winter stew when the temperature begins to drop. This rich dish and its thick, tasty gravy really hits the spot. With tender oyster mushrooms, caramelized carrots and onions, as well as a good helping of red wine and miso for umami-packed flavours, this has quickly become one of my most popular recipes – somewhat beef bourguignon, but without the beef.

Serve it with creamy **Mashed Potatoes & Long-stem Broccoli [1]** for a classic winter dinner. Then turn it into a dreamy pasta sauce – **Rich Winter Ragu with Pappardelle [2]** – so quick, so simple. Transform leftovers into **Winter Pie & Garlic Green Beans [3]** by popping a pastry lid on top and baking it to golden-brown perfection. The garlicky green beans add the perfect crunch.

Preheat the oven to 160°C/140°C fan/400°F/gas 3.

Heat the oil in a large ovenproof pot over a medium heat. Add the carrots and shallots, then increase the heat and cook for 6 minutes until slightly caramelized and brown. Add the mushrooms, bay leaves and fresh thyme, and cook for another 2 minutes. Sprinkle over the flour and mix to combine, then pour in the red wine. Increase the heat to high and cook, stirring now and then, until the wine is reduced by half, roughly 3 minutes.

Add the tomatoes, sweet potatoes, vegetable stock and miso paste and mix to combine. Season to taste with salt and a generous amount of black pepper.

Transfer to the oven with the lid on and cook for 40 minutes, until the carrots have softened. Top with fresh parsley.

The stew is now ready to be used in the recipes on pages 68–71, or it will keep in the fridge for 3 days, or in the freezer for 3 months.

Mashed Potatoes
& Long-stem
Broccoli

Option
One

Serves 2

~~~

2 portions of Winter Stew (page 66)

1 tbsp olive oil

200g (7oz) long-stem broccoli

<div style="writing-mode: vertical">MASHED POTATO</div>

4 (about 500g/17½oz) white potatoes (such as King Edwards or Maris Piper), peeled and chopped into even chunks

2 tbsp vegan butter

2 tbsp nutritional yeast (optional)

sea salt and freshly ground black pepper

Place the potatoes in a large saucepan over a high heat and add enough water to cover them by 2.5cm (1in). Bring to the boil, then add a pinch of salt and cook for 25 minutes until tender.

Meanwhile, warm the winter stew in a saucepan over a high heat. Bring to the boil, then reduce the heat to low and simmer for 6 minutes. If it begins to thicken, add a splash of water.

To make the broccoli, heat the oil in a frying pan over a medium heat. Add the broccoli, season with salt and pepper and cook for 5 minutes, tossing occasionally, until tender.

Drain the potatoes, then mash with a potato masher until fluffy. Add the vegan butter and nutritional yeast (if using), season to taste with salt and pepper, and stir to combine.

Serve the mashed potatoes with the winter stew and broccoli.

Rich Winter Ragu with Pappardelle

Option
Two

Serves 2

~~~

250g (9oz) pappardelle

2 portions of Winter Stew (page 66)

sea salt and freshly ground black pepper

<span style="writing-mode: vertical;">TO SERVE</span>

handful of fresh flat-leaf parsley

2 tbsp nutritional yeast (optional)

2 tbsp extra-virgin olive oil

Cook the pasta in a large pot of salted boiling water according to the packet instructions until al dente. When ready, reserve a cupful of the cooking water, then drain the pasta as usual and set aside.

Heat the winter stew in a deep saucepan over a medium heat for 5 minutes until piping hot. Add the pappardelle and a splash of the reserved pasta water and mix well.

Divide between 2 plates. Scatter over the fresh parsley and nutritional yeast (if using), add a few twists of pepper, then drizzle over the olive oil and serve.

Winter Pie & Garlic Green Beans

Option
Three

Serves 2

~~

2 portions of Winter Stew (page 66)

1 sheet of ready-made shortcrust pastry

flour, for dusting

1 tbsp olive oil

1 tsp maple syrup

GREEN BEANS

1 tbsp olive oil

200g (7oz) green beans, trimmed

2 garlic cloves, minced

sea salt

Preheat the oven to 200°C/180°C fan/400°F/gas 6 (or follow the shortcrust pastry package instructions).

Place the stew in a small but deep roasting tin or oven dish that's appropriate for a pie.

Roll out the pastry on a lightly floured surface until 5mm (¼in) thick. Brush around the edge of the roasting tin or dish with water, then lay the pastry over it and press it down to make it stick. Use a sharp knife to trim off any excess pastry, then press around the edges with a fork. Cut a steam hole in the middle. Mix the olive oil and maple syrup in a small bowl, then brush this mixture over the pastry. Place in the oven and bake for 30 minutes until golden brown.

Meanwhile, prepare the green beans. Heat the olive oil in a frying pan over a medium heat. Add the green beans and garlic, season with salt and cook, stirring occasionally, for 6 minutes until the beans are tender but still have a slight bite.

Serve the beans alongside the pie for a warming winter meal.

Stewed Berries

Makes 4 servings

600g (1lb 3oz) mixed berries
(fresh or frozen)

6 tbsp maple syrup (or sweetener
of your choice)

freshly grated lemon zest

Here is the perfect recipe for fresh berries in season, or for when you have frozen berries in the freezer that need eating. Granted, the three ways of using them make more than 2 servings because baking dishes aren't small enough for 2 – probably a good thing, because recipes like these deserve to be made for more people to enjoy. You can also cook these recipes with any seasonal fruit.

For a comforting, quick and easy pudding for the family, try the **Mixed Berry Cobbler [1]**. Be sure to serve immediately with a scoop of vegan vanilla ice cream to melt over the top. To make **Mixed Berry Chia Jam [2]**, simply add omega-rich chia seeds – a hero food of mine – to your berries and watch them thicken into a super-tasty, nutritious jam! Spread on toast or banana bread, or add a generous spoonful to overnight oats or porridge, or use wherever you fancy some jam. My indulgent **No-bake Berry Coconut Cake [3]** is incredibly creamy and smooth. No baking involved – just freeze to set, then serve within 10 minutes for the perfect texture.

Place the berries in a deep saucepan over a low heat. Stir in the maple syrup and a touch of lemon zest. Simmer for 10 minutes, stirring occasionally.

The stewed berries are now ready to be used in the recipes on pages 74–7, or will keep in the fridge for up to 5 days, or the freezer for up to 3 months.

Mixed Berry Cobbler

Option One

Serves 6

130g (4¾oz) plain flour

100g (3½oz) golden caster sugar

2 tsp baking powder

180ml (6fl oz) plant-based milk

2 portions of Stewed Berries (page 72)

1 tbsp cornflour

115g (4oz) vegan butter

sea salt

4 scoops of vegan vanilla ice cream, to serve

Preheat oven to 200°C/180°C fan/400°F/gas 6.

Place the flour, sugar, baking powder and a pinch of salt in a large bowl and mix together. Add the plant-based milk and stir to form a batter.

Place the stewed berries in a separate bowl. Add the cornflour and mix until well combined.

Put the vegan butter in a 15 x 25cm (6 x 10in) baking tray (about 1 litre capacity) and place in the oven for a few minutes, until the butter has melted. Remove the tray from the oven and pour in the batter mixture, using a spatula to spread it into the corners. Top with the stewed berries, then bake 40–45 minutes. The cobbler should be slightly golden and should spring back when you touch it.

Serve warm with big scoops of vegan vanilla ice cream.

Mixed Berry Chia Jam

Option Two

Makes 300g (10½ oz) jar

2 portions of Stewed Berries (page 72)

1–3 tbsp maple syrup

4 tbsp chia seeds

Place the stewed berries in a saucepan over a low heat and warm for 6 minutes until piping hot. Turn off the heat, add a tablespoon of maple syrup, then taste and add more if needed to achieve your preferred sweetness. Mix in the chia seeds and 4 tablespoons water. Leave the mixture to rest off the heat for 10 minutes, stirring occasionally. The chia seeds will start to absorb the liquid, leaving you with a thick jam.

You can store the jam in an airtight container in the fridge for up to 5 days.

No-bake Berry Coconut Cake

Option Three

Serves 6

200g (7oz) cashew nuts, soaked in water for 1 hour, then drained

2 portions of Stewed Berries (page 72)

1 tbsp cornflour

1–3 tbsp maple syrup or sweetener of choice

50ml (1¾fl oz) lemon juice

80ml (2¾fl oz) coconut oil

80ml (2¾fl oz) maple syrup

160ml (5½fl oz) full-fat coconut milk

1 tsp vanilla extract

Pinch of sea salt

BASE

120g (4¼oz) walnuts or mixed nuts

200g (7oz) dates, pitted

Pinch of sea salt

Make sure your cashews are soaking for the required time before you start. Line a 15cm (6in) baking dish with baking paper.

Place the stewed berries in a saucepan over a low heat. Sprinkle in the cornflour and simmer, stirring now and then, for about 5 minutes until the mixture thickens. Turn off the heat, add a tablespoon of maple syrup, then taste and add more if needed to achieve your preferred sweetness.

To make the base, place the walnuts in a blender and blitz into small crumbs. Transfer to a plate, then add the dates and a pinch of salt to the blender and blitz into small pieces. Return the walnuts to the blender and pulse just until combined with the dates – don't overmix or it will turn into butter. Transfer the mixture to a plate, then rinse out the blender.

Put the drained cashew nuts in the clean blender, then add the lemon juice, coconut oil, maple syrup, coconut milk, vanilla extract and a pinch of sea salt. Blend until completely smooth.

Place the walnut and date mixture in the lined baking dish, pressing it down with your fingers to create an even base. Pour the cashew mixture over the top.

Place in the freezer for 2 hours to set, then pour the stewed berries on top. Return to the freezer for another 2 hours.

Serve within 10 minutes of removing from the freezer for the best texture.

Wholesome, flavourful food that makes you feel good is worth celebrating. Nothing beats sitting down with a delicious meal and taking the time to enjoy it.

Rachel Ama

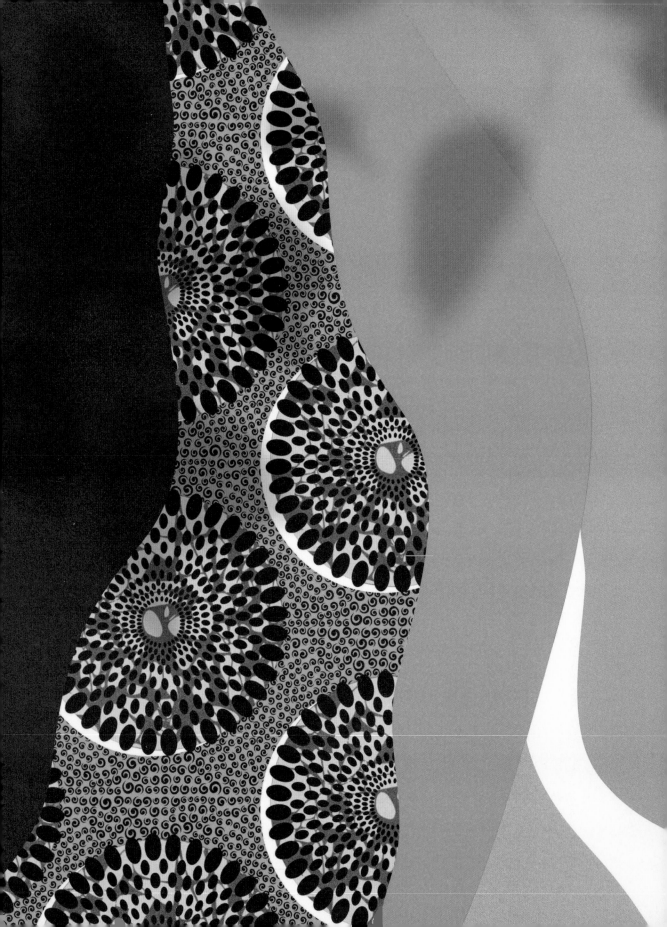

One
Pan

Chapter Two

Thai Basil Plant-based Mince

Main
Recipe

1 tbsp coconut oil

3 garlic cloves, finely sliced

2 spring onions, finely sliced

½ red chilli, finely chopped

1 red pepper, sliced

500g (1lb 2oz) vegan mince

1 tbsp brown rice miso paste
(optional, see method)

handful of fresh Thai basil leaves

SAUCE

3 tbsp fresh lime juice

3 tbsp soy sauce

4 tsp rice vinegar

2 tbsp maple syrup

This super-quick, plant-based mince dish is inspired by Thai street food. A generous splash of soy sauce, sharp vinegar and sweet maple syrup create a delicious, salty, slightly caramel sauce that coats the mince, which is mixed with a generous handful of aromatic fresh Thai basil for a spicy kick with hints of liquorice. If you can't find Thai basil, you can use regular basil.

Enjoy this with **Brown Rice & Butter Lettuce Salad [1]**, which includes avocado, spring onions and chilli flakes, tossed in a sesame vinaigrette. Mix any leftovers with short sushi rice, kimchi, crunchy carrots and cucumber to make a quick and easy **Teriyaki Bibimbap Bowl [2]**. It makes the perfect base for a slightly sweet and nutty **Hoisin Mince Stir-fry [3]**. Just combine your mince with noodles and crunchy Chinese cabbage – the ultimate comfort food.

To prepare the sauce, simply add all the ingredients to a bowl and mix until combined into a smooth sauce. Set aside until needed.

Heat the oil in a wok or large frying pan over a medium heat. Add the garlic, spring onions, chilli and red pepper, increase the heat to high heat and stir-fry for 1 minute.

Add the vegan mince and mix well. Reduce the heat to medium and pour in the sauce, stirring to combine. Cook until the mixture is piping hot. Different vegan mince brands can vary: if the mince has absorbed all the sauce, you can mix the miso paste with 5 tablespoons water and stir this in too. Stir in the Thai basil leaves.

The mince is now ready to be used in the recipes on pages 85–6, or it will keep in the fridge for 3 days (check your mince packet instructions), or in the freezer for 3 months.

Brown Rice & Butter Lettuce Salad

Option One

Serves 2

~~~

200g (7oz) brown rice, rinsed well under cold running water

2 portions of Thai Basil Mince (page 82)

2 heads of butter lettuce, leaves separated

1 avocado, peeled, stoned and sliced

1 spring onion, finely sliced

1 tbsp sesame seeds

1 tsp red chilli flakes

handful of fresh Thai basil leaves

DRESSING

4 tbsp soy sauce

2 tbsp rice vinegar

2 tsp sesame oil

1 tsp dried red chilli flakes

1 tbsp fresh lime juice

1½ tbsp maple syrup

Place the rice in a pan over a high heat and cover with 500ml (18fl oz) salted water. Bring to the boil, then reduce the heat, cover and leave to cook for 45 minutes, or until all the water has been absorbed.

Meanwhile, place the Thai basil mince in a saucepan over a medium heat for 5 minutes, stirring occasionally, until piping hot.

Combine all the dressing ingredients and mix well. Arrange the lettuce on a serving platter with the cooked rice and Thai basil mince. Drizzle over the dressing and top with the avocado, spring onions, sesame seeds, chilli flakes and Thai basil leaves.

Teriyaki Mince Bibimbap Bowl

Option Two

Serves 2

~~~

190g (6¾oz) short-grain sushi rice, rinsed in cold running water

2 portions of Thai Basil Mince (page 82)

2 tbsp teriyaki sauce

¼ cucumber, sliced

1 carrot, grated

4 tbsp kimchi

1 spring onion, finely sliced

handful of fresh coriander, roughly chopped

1 tsp sesame seeds

2 tsp sriracha or gochujang sauce

lime wedges, to serve

Place the rice in a saucepan with 300ml (10fl oz) cold water. Leave to soak for 30 minutes.

When the time is up, place the saucepan over a high heat and bring to the boil, then cover with a lid, reduce the heat to low and simmer for 10 minutes, or until all the water has been absorbed. Set aside, still covered, for 10 minutes.

Place the Thai basil mince in a saucepan over a medium heat for 5 minutes, stirring occasionally. Add the teriyaki sauce and cook for 2 more minutes, stirring, until the mince is piping hot. Remove from the heat.

To serve, arrange the rice and mince in 2 bowls, along with the cucumber, carrot and kimchi. Scatter over the spring onion, coriander and sesame seeds, add a drizzle of sriracha and serve with lime wedges for squeezing over.

Hoisin Mince
Stir-fry

Option
Three

Serves 2

130g (4½oz) thin wheat noodles

1 tbsp coconut oil

1 red onion, sliced

2 portions of Thai Basil Mince
(page 82)

2 garlic cloves, finely chopped

½ Chinese cabbage, shredded

1 carrot, shredded

SAUCE

1 tbsp hoisin sauce

1 tbsp soy sauce

1 tsp mirin

TO SERVE

2 spring onions, finely chopped

1 tbsp sesame seeds

2 tbsp peanut oil (or sesame oil)

lime wedges

Cook the noodles in a large pan of boiling water until al dente – it's always better to undercook than overcook. Drain the noodles and run under cold water to stop the cooking process, then set aside.

Mix the sauce ingredients together in a small bowl and set aside.

Heat the coconut oil in a large frying pan or wok over a high heat. Add the red onion and stir-fry for 1 minute, then add the Thai basil mince and garlic. Stir and toss around until the mince is piping hot. Add the cabbage and carrot, and stir-fry for 30 seconds. Finally, add the noodles and sauce and cook for 1 minute more, mixing well to combine.

Divide between 2 plates or bowls and scatter over the spring onions and sesame seeds. Drizzle with a little peanut oil and serve with lime wedges, for squeezing over.

Caribbean-style Ackee

Makes 4 servings

1 tbsp coconut oil

1 red pepper, sliced

1 red onion, finely sliced

2 spring onions, finely sliced

1 red chilli, finely diced

3 garlic cloves, minced

2 plum tomatoes, roughly chopped

1 tbsp soy sauce

2 fresh thyme sprigs

1 x 540g (1lb 3oz) can ackee, drained and rinsed

1 lime, halved

handful of fresh coriander

Ackee, the national fruit of Jamaica, is eaten throughout the Caribbean and has a neutral, buttery flavour and a light and soft texture. When cooked right, it makes a really tasty alternative to scrambled egg. This recipe combines the freshness of tomatoes with the creaminess of ackee for a succulent, savoury bite with a hint of spice and fresh herbs. Eat on a Sunday afternoon with a cup of tea or freshly pressed juice, preferably soursop, but orange juice will do too!

For my favourite Caribbean-style breakfast/lunch, enjoy the ackee with **Roast Plantain and Caribbean-style Kale [1]**, which is reminiscent of callaloo. You can also spin it into really tasty and comforting **Breakfast Burritos [2]** served with avocado, salsa and a likkle hot sauce in a lightly toasted tortilla wrap. Making fried rice is a super-easy way to use up any veggies that need to be eaten, so my third option is to mix the ackee into a quick **Ackee Fried Rice [3]** that includes garlic, ginger, soy sauce and broccoli – or any other veggies you have in the fridge.

Heat the coconut oil in a frying pan over a medium heat, add the red pepper, onion, spring onion and chilli and cook for 5 minutes, stirring occasionally, until softened. Add the garlic, tomatoes, soy sauce and fresh thyme and cook for a further 4 minutes, stirring occasionally.

Finally, add the ackee, mixing it in gently and being very careful to keep the pieces whole and not let them get mushy. Cover and cook for 4 minutes to warm the ackee, then remove from the heat.

Serve with a squeeze of lime juice and a sprinkling of fresh coriander.

The ackee is now ready to be served with the recipes on pages 90–2, or will keep in the fridge for 3 days.

Roast Plantain & Caribbean-style Sautéed Kale

Option
One

Serves 2

1 ripe plantain, peeled, halved and sliced lengthways

1 tsp olive oil

1 tbsp coconut oil

1 red onion, finely diced

1 red chilli, sliced

3 garlic cloves, minced

1 tsp smoked paprika

2 plum tomatoes, chopped

200g (7oz) kale, any woody stalks removed

1 tbsp soy sauce

1 tsp liquid smoke (if you can't find this, use soy sauce)

2 portions of Caribbean-style Ackee (page 88)

2 slices of sourdough bread

1 tbsp vegan butter or extra-virgin olive oil

1 avocado, peeled, stoned and sliced

handful of fresh parsley, chopped

Preheat the oven to 220°C/200°C fan/425°F/gas 7.

Lay the plantain slices in a roasting tray and drizzle with the olive oil. Roast for 20 minutes, turning over halfway through, until golden brown and tender.

Meanwhile, heat the coconut oil in a frying pan over a medium heat. Add the onion and cook for 3 minutes, then add the chilli, garlic and paprika. Stir to combine and cook for another 3 minutes. Now add the tomatoes, kale, soy sauce and liquid smoke. Cook for 5 minutes, stirring, until the kale has wilted.

Put the Caribbean-style ackee in a frying pan over a medium heat, cover and warm for 5 minutes, until piping hot.

Toast the bread, then spread with the vegan butter. Serve alongside the ackee, roasted plantain, sautéed kale and sliced avocado. Sprinkle with fresh parsley to serve.

Ackee
Breakfast
Burrito

Option
Two

Serves 2

～～

2 portions of Caribbean-style
Ackee (page 88)

2 large tortilla wraps

1 avocado, peeled, stoned and sliced

handful of spinach

handful of fresh coriander, chopped

6 cherry tomatoes, sliced

2 tbsp chipotle sauce or hot sauce

Place the ackee in a saucepan over a high heat for about 4 minutes, stirring carefully now and then, until piping hot.

Heat the wraps in a frying pan over a medium heat for 2 minutes on each side.

To assemble your burritos, lay each wrap on a plate and add half the hot ackee, then some avocado, spinach, coriander and cherry tomatoes. Finish with a drizzle of chipotle sauce or hot sauce, and roll up into a burrito.

Ackee
Fried Rice

Option
Three

Serves 2

~~

200g (7oz) basmati rice, rinsed well under cold running water
1 tbsp coconut oil
½ head of broccoli, roughly chopped
thumb-sized piece of fresh root ginger, grated
2 garlic cloves, minced
1 red chilli, seeded and finely sliced
1 tbsp soy sauce
2 portions of Caribbean-style Ackee (page 88)
handful of fresh coriander, chopped
lime wedges, to serve

Place the rice in a deep saucepan over a high heat and cover with 390ml (13¾fl oz) water. Season with salt and bring to the boil, then reduce the heat to low. Cover and leave to cook for 10 minutes, or until all the water has been absorbed. Remove from the heat and fluff up the rice with a fork.

Heat the coconut oil in a wok or large frying pan over a high heat. Add the broccoli, ginger, garlic and chilli and cook for 3 minutes, then add the cooked rice and soy sauce, stirring quickly to combine. Add the ackee, and cook, stirring, until piping hot.

Serve scattered with fresh coriander, offering lime wedges on the side for squeezing over.

Sticky Miso Oyster Mushrooms

Main
Recipe

Makes 4 servings

1 tbsp olive oil

500g (1lb 2oz) oyster mushrooms

sea salt

1 tbsp Chinese five spice

STICKY MISO SAUCE

2 tbsp brown rice miso

4 tbsp water

2 tbsp rice vinegar

2 tbsp maple syrup

2 tbsp light soy sauce

½ tsp chilli flakes

1½ tsp cornflour

Crispy edges, tender centres seasoned in Chinese five spice and smothered in a sweet miso sauce, these sticky oyster mushrooms are really quick to make, packed with flavour and incredibly addictive!

To make my **Greens Stir-fry [1]**, serve the mushrooms with stir-fried pak choi, green beans and mangetout in a chilli and ginger sauce, with some brown rice and topped with toasted sesame seeds. Or toss them in a wok with sesame **Soba Noodles [2]** for a quick and easy delicious dinner. Refresh leftovers to make a vegan version of a traditional Vietnamese **Bahn Mi Sandwich [3]** – sticky miso oyster mushrooms layered with pickled carrots, spring onions, vegan mayo and sriracha on a soft white baguette.

Heat the oil in a large saucepan over a medium–high heat. Add the oyster mushrooms and cook for 7 minutes, pressing down on them with a spatula to release excess juices. Season with salt and Chinese five spice, then flip over and cook for another 7 minutes, until the mushrooms begin to caramelize and turn brown. Remove the mushrooms from the pan and roughly chop.

Return the pan to a medium heat and add the sauce ingredients apart from the cornflour. Mix the cornflour and 1½ tablespoons water in a small cup or bowl to make a slurry. Once the sauce is hot, stir in the cornflour mixture, then cook for a few minutes until the sauce thickens. Return the mushrooms to the pan and stir for 1 minute to coat them in the sauce and they are piping hot.

The mushrooms are now ready to be used in the recipes on pages 96–9, or will keep in the fridge for 3 days.

Sticky Miso Mushrooms & Greens Stir-fry

Option One

Serves 2

200g (7oz) brown rice, rinsed well under cold running water

1 tbsp coconut oil

1 red chilli, sliced

thumb-sized piece of fresh root ginger, sliced into thin matchsticks

2 garlic cloves, sliced

100g (3½oz) mangetout

2 baby pak choi, quartered

100g (3½oz) green beans, trimmed

100g (3½oz) long-stem broccoli

1 tbsp soy sauce

2 portions of Sticky Miso Oyster Mushrooms (page 94)

TO SERVE

1 tsp toasted sesame seeds

handful of fresh coriander, chopped

1 lime, cut into wedges

Place the rice in a deep saucepan over a high heat and cover with 500ml (18fl oz) water. Season with salt and bring to the boil, then reduce the heat to low. Cover and leave to cook for 45 minutes, or until all the water has been absorbed. Remove from the heat and fluff up the rice with a fork.

Meanwhile, heat the oil in a wok over a medium–high heat. Add the chilli, ginger and garlic, and cook for 1 minute, stirring. Add the mangetout, pak choi, green beans and broccoli, and stir-fry for 5 minutes, until cooked but still vibrant in colour. Add the soy sauce and stir to combine.

Push the veg to the side of the wok and add the mushrooms, heating for 3 minutes, until piping hot.

Scatter the toasted sesame seeds and fresh coriander over the mushrooms. Serve with the greens stir-fry, the rice and lime wedges on the side, for squeezing over.

Miso Mushroom
Soba Noodles

Option
Two

Serves 2

200g (7oz) soba noodles

1 tbsp coconut oil

100g (3½oz) long-stem broccoli

thumb-sized piece of fresh root ginger, finely chopped

2 garlic cloves, finely chopped

2 portions of Sticky Miso Oyster Mushrooms (page 94)

SAUCE

1 tbsp sesame oil

1 tbsp soy sauce

1 tsp maple syrup

1 tsp rice vinegar

TO SERVE

1 tbsp toasted sesame seeds

2 spring onions, finely chopped

1 tbsp chilli flakes

handful of fresh coriander, chopped

1 lime, cut into wedges

Place the noodles in a large bowl of freshly boiled water and leave to soften for a few minutes, or according to the packet instructions. You want them to be slightly undercooked. Drain and rinse under cold water to stop the cooking process, then set aside until needed.

To make the sauce, place all the ingredients for it in a small bowl or jug and mix well.

Heat the oil in a wok over a medium-high heat. Add the broccoli and stir-fry for 3–4 minutes until starting to soften but still vibrant in colour, then add the ginger and garlic and cook for 1 minute, then add the noodles. Pour over the sauce and stir-fry for 2 minutes, tossing to combine.

Push the veg and noodles to the side of the wok and add the mushrooms, heating for 3 minutes, until piping hot.

Serve the noodles alongside the mushrooms, with toasted sesame seeds, sliced spring onions, chilli flakes and fresh coriander scattered over the top, and lime wedges on the side, for squeezing over.

Bahn Mi Sandwich

/ Option
Three

Serves 2

~~~

2 small baguettes

4 tbsp vegan mayonnaise

2 portions of Sticky Miso Oyster Mushrooms (page 94)

¼ cucumber, sliced into ribbons

2 spring onions, sliced

handful of fresh coriander, chopped

1 red chilli, seeded and finely sliced

2 tsp sriracha sauce

PICKLED CARROTS

3 tbsp rice vinegar

1 tbsp sugar

2 carrots, sliced into ribbons

First make the pickled carrots: combine the rice vinegar and sugar in a bowl along with 1 tablespoon water and mix together. Add the carrot ribbons and rub the pickling mixture into them. Set aside for at least 15 minutes.

Slice open the baguettes, spread with the vegan mayonnaise, then layer some sticky mushrooms, pickled carrots, cucumber and spring onions inside. Top with a generous amount of coriander, the chilli and a touch of sriracha, and enjoy.

Cajun Beer-battered Oyster Mushrooms

with Tartare Sauce

Main
Recipe

Makes 4 servings

150g (5½oz) plain flour

½ tsp baking powder

2 tsp sweet paprika

½ tsp cayenne pepper

1 tsp ground white pepper

1 tsp ground cumin

1 tsp dried oregano

½ tsp dried thyme

1 tsp garlic powder

2 tsp salt, plus extra to serve

50g (1¾oz) cornflour

300g (10½oz) oyster mushrooms,
torn into bite-sized pieces

sunflower or olive oil, for frying

320ml (11fl oz) cold lager
(or soda water)

lemon wedges, to serve

TARTARE SAUCE

100g (3½oz) vegan mayonnaise

2 tbsp capers, finely chopped

1 garlic clove, minced

freshly ground black pepper

handful of fresh flat-leaf parsley

This is inspired by my time in New Orleans, where I tucked into a lot of different Cajun-spiced fried foods. Your mind will be blown by the succulent texture of the mushrooms in their crisp flavoured batter. This is a top recipe for epic street food made at home! If you like, you can switch up the spices or keep it simply beer-battered.

First up, I've served the mushrooms with crisp **Garlicky Crushed New Potatoes [1]** topped with fresh herbs and a dollop of tangy tartare sauce. You can refresh your leftovers in an **American-style 'Chicken' Pickle Sandwich [2]** with gherkins, tartare sauce and lettuce in a soft burger bun. For something speedy, pop these fried mushrooms into warm tortillas to create **Cajun Tacos with Pickled Red Onion & Tartare Sauce [3]**.

To make the tartare sauce, mix all the ingredients for it in a bowl, then set aside.

Mix the flour, baking powder and all the seasonings together in a large bowl. Place the cornflour in a separate bowl or on a large plate, and place the mushrooms in a third bowl.

Pour a 2cm (1in) depth of oil into a deep frying pan or wok and place over a high heat until it registers 180°C (356°F) on a thermometer. Alternatively, test the temperature by dipping the end of a wooden spoon in it – if it's hot enough for frying, the oil should bubble around it. Be careful not to overheat the oil or it will begin to smoke.

Whisk the cold beer or soda water into the seasoned flour mixture to make a batter. Then, working quickly, take a piece of oyster

mushroom and dip it in the cornflour. Shake off any excess, then dip it in the beer batter before carefully transferring it to the hot oil. Working in batches, cook for 3–4 minutes, or until each piece is golden and crisp. Once cooked, drain the mushrooms on a wire rack or a plate lined with kitchen paper. Season with extra salt and squeeze over a little fresh lemon.

The mushrooms are now ready to be used in the recipes on pages 104–7, or will keep in the fridge for 3 days.

Garlicky Crushed New Potatoes

Option One

Serves 2

200g (7oz) new potatoes

3 tbsp olive oil

2 garlic cloves, sliced

2 portions of Cajun Beer-battered Oyster Mushrooms (page 102)

2 portions of Tartare Sauce (page 102)

squeeze of lemon juice

handful of fresh flat-leaf parsley

1 spring onion, finely chopped

sea salt and freshly ground black pepper

Preheat the oven to 200°C/180°C fan/425°F/gas 6.

Place a pan of water over a high heat and bring to the boil. Add the potatoes and cook for 15 minutes until tender, then drain.

Lightly grease a baking sheet with a little of the oil, then lay out the potatoes in a single layer. Use a fork to carefully crush and flatten each potato while keeping it in one piece. Scatter over the garlic, drizzle with the remaining oil and season with salt and pepper. Roast for 20–25 minutes until golden brown.

Remove the potatoes from the oven, turn up the heat and quickly place the battered mushrooms on a wire rack over a baking tray and bake for 5 minutes, or until warmed through and crispy.

Serve the mushrooms with the new potatoes, a spoonful of tartare sauce, a squeeze of fresh lemon juice, and a sprinkling of fresh parsley and spring onion.

American-style 'Chicken' Pickle Sandwich

Option Two

Serves 2

2 portions of Cajun Beer-battered Oyster Mushrooms (page 102)

2 portions of Tartare Sauce (page 102)

2 vegan brioche burger buns, sliced in half

2 gherkins, sliced

2 tbsp sriracha or your favourite hot sauce

handful of lettuce, shredded

Preheat the oven to 240°C/220°C fan/475°F/gas 9.

Place the battered mushrooms on a wire rack over a baking tray and bake for 5 minutes. Check to see if they're warmed through and crispy. If not, return them to the oven for another few minutes.

To build your sandwich, spread the tartare sauce on the bottom half of your brioche bun. Pile on the mushrooms, then top with the gherkins, hot sauce and lettuce. Serve immediately.

Cajun Tacos with Pickled Red Onion & Tartare Sauce

Option Three

Serves 2

2 portions of Cajun Beer-battered Oyster Mushrooms (page 102)

4 tortilla wraps

1 avocado, peeled, stoned and sliced

handful of lettuce leaves

handful of fresh coriander

2 portions of Tartare Sauce (page 102)

4 tbsp sriracha or your favourite hot sauce

PICKLED RED ONION

1 red onion, finely sliced

1 tbsp apple cider vinegar

1 tsp sea salt

Preheat the oven to 240°C/220°C fan/475°F/gas 9.

Meanwhile, make the pickled onion. Place the sliced red onion in a bowl and pour over the vinegar. Add the salt, stir to combine, then set aside for at least 10 minutes.

Place the battered mushrooms on a wire rack over a baking tray and bake for 5 minutes. Check to see if they're warmed through and crispy. If not, return them to the oven for another few minutes.

Warm the tortillas in a frying pan over a medium heat for 2 minutes on each side.

To assemble the tacos, place each wrap on a plate and pile the battered mushrooms on them. Top with the avocado, lettuce and coriander, then drizzle over some tartare sauce and sriracha. Fold the wraps over and serve.

Jerk-spiced Lentils

Makes 4 servings

1 tbsp olive oil

1 red onion, sliced

thumb-sized piece of fresh root ginger, grated

1½ tbsp jerk seasoning

1 tbsp maple syrup

1 tbsp tomato purée

4 garlic cloves, finely sliced

4 large tomatoes, quartered

300g (10½oz) dried Puy lentils

800ml (1½ pints) vegetable stock

½ Scotch bonnet chilli, seeded

2 fresh thyme sprigs

handful of fresh coriander, chopped

2 spring onions, sliced

sea salt and freshly ground black pepper

Jerk spices are among my favourite flavours: whenever I smell a likkle jerk seasoning, it feels like a big warm hug. Jerk seasoning is not limited to use with meat – trust me, you can still enjoy those flavours in fun plant-based ways. In this recipe, the dried lentils absorb the jerk spices and flavours for a seriously delicious dish.

First up, serve with slightly sweet and nutty **Coconut Rice, Patacones & Pineapple Salsa [1]**. Patacones are fried green plantains squashed into a patty, then fried again and sprinkled in flaky salt – yum! For a super-quick meal, mix fresh pasta with a sprinkling of parsley and nutritional yeast to create **Jerk Lentil Spaghetti [2]**. Lastly, serve with really simple **Plantain Rotis & Salad [3]**. These use just flour, boiled plantain and a pinch of salt to create a dough, which is then cooked in a hot pan. Scoop up the hot jerk spiced lentils with these soft plantain rotis, and add a fresh salad on the side. You can also use this recipe to fill the patties on page 40.

Heat the oil in a deep frying pan over a medium heat. Add the onion and sauté for 5 minutes until softened and slightly browned. Now add the ginger, jerk seasoning, maple syrup, tomato purée and garlic. Sauté for another 3 minutes, then add the tomatoes, lentils, vegetable stock, chilli and thyme. Season with salt and black pepper. Bring to the boil, then reduce the heat to a simmer and cook for 30 minutes, until the lentils have softened. Sprinkle fresh coriander and spring onions on top.

The lentils are now ready to be used in the recipes on pages 110–13, or will keep in the fridge for 3 days, or in the freezer for 3 months.

Coconut Rice, Patacones & Pineapple Salsa

Option One

Serves 2

2 portions of Jerk-spiced Lentils (page 108)

COCONUT RICE

200g (7oz) basmati rice, rinsed well under running water

240ml (8¼fl oz) coconut milk

sea salt

PINEAPPLE SALSA

½ ripe pineapple, peeled and chopped into 5mm (¼in) chunks

1 tsp extra-virgin olive oil

1 tbsp fresh lime juice

60g (2¼oz) fresh coriander, roughly chopped

¼ red onion, finely sliced

1 large tomato, diced

PATACONES

2–4 tbsp olive oil

2 green plantains, peeled and sliced into 4cm (1½in) chunks

Begin by making the coconut rice. Place the rice and coconut milk in a large saucepan. Add 200ml (7fl oz) water, then season with salt and stir to combine. Place over a medium heat and bring to a simmer, then cover, reduce the heat to low and cook for a further 10 minutes, or until all the liquid has been absorbed. Remove the lid and fluff the rice with a fork.

To make the salsa, place all the ingredients for it in a bowl and mix well. Set aside until needed.

Place the jerk-spiced lentils in a saucepan over a medium heat and bring to the boil. Reduce the heat to low and simmer for 6 minutes, stirring occasionally, until piping hot. Add a splash of water if the lentils begin to thicken.

Meanwhile, to make the patacones, place the oil in a large, deep saucepan over a high heat. When hot, add the plantain slices and fry on each side for 5 minutes. Drain them on kitchen paper, then use a rolling pin or plate to flatten each slice to a thickness of about 5mm (¼in).

Once flat, return the slices to the pan and fry once more for about 2 minutes on each side, until crunchy. Transfer to a plate lined with kitchen paper to absorb any excess oil. Season with sea salt while still hot.

To serve, divide the rice between 2 plates and add your lentils, patacones and salsa.

Jerk Lentil Spaghetti

Option
Two

Serves 2

250g (9oz) spaghetti

2 portions of Jerk-spiced Lentils
(page 108)

sea salt and freshly ground black
pepper

TO SERVE

1 tbsp extra-virgin olive oil

handful of fresh curly leaf parsley

2 tbsp nutritional yeast

Cook the spaghetti in a large pan of salted boiling water according to the packet instructions until al dente. When ready, reserve a cupful of the cooking water, then drain the pasta as usual and return it to the pan.

Add the jerk-spiced lentils to the spaghetti and mix together over a low heat. Add a splash of the reserved pasta water to loosen, and cook for 2 minutes, until the lentils are warmed through and everything is completely combined.

Divide the pasta between 2 plates or bowls and drizzle with the olive oil. Scatter over some parsley and nutritional yeast, season with salt and black pepper to taste and serve.

Plantain Rotis & Salad

Option
Three

Serves 2

2 portions of Jerk-spiced Lentils
(page 108)

handful of fresh coriander, chopped

1 tsp chilli flakes

2 tbsp unsweetened coconut
yoghurt

PLANTAIN ROTIS

200g (7oz) green plantain
(usually one), peeled and
chopped into chunks

150g plain flour, plus extra
for dusting

1 tbsp olive oil

sea salt

SALAD

2 large tomatoes, sliced

½ red onion, sliced

200g (7oz) mixed salad leaves

1 avocado, peeled, stoned and sliced

1 lime, halved

1 tbsp extra-virgin olive oil

To make the rotis, bring a deep pan of water to the boil. Add the plantain chunks and cook for 8 minutes until completely soft. Drain and transfer to a bowl. Using a potato masher or a fork, mash the plantain to form a smooth purée.

Place the flour in a separate bowl and season with salt, stirring to combine. Add the mashed plantain and mix to form a ball of dough. If the mixture is too sticky, add a pinch more flour. The texture will really depend on how ripe the plantain is and how much moisture it contains. Once you're happy with the texture, divide the dough into 4 equal pieces.

Lightly dust a clean surface with flour, then use a rolling pin to roll out each piece as thinly as possible without breaking the dough. If necessary, dust the rolling pin with flour to prevent it sticking.

Meanwhile, place the jerk-spiced lentils in a saucepan over a medium heat and bring to the boil. Reduce the heat to low and simmer for 6 minutes, stirring occasionally, until piping hot. Add a splash of water if the lentils begin to thicken.

Now combine all the salad ingredients in a bowl and mix well.

Heat the oil in a large frying pan over a medium-high heat, then cook the rotis one at a time for 3 minutes on each side, until brown. Transfer to a plate and keep warm while you cook the remaining rotis. These are best eaten fresh and hot, so serve immediately.

To serve, take a roti and fill it with the lentils and drizzle with coconut yoghurt. Sprinkle over some coriander and chilli flakes and serve the salad on the side.

Cuban Black Beans

Main
Recipe

Makes 4 servings

1–2 tbsp olive oil

1 onion, chopped

1 green pepper, chopped

1 tsp ground cumin

2 tsp paprika

1 tsp dried oregano

1 tbsp tomato purée

2 bay leaves

350g (12½oz) dried black beans,
soaked overnight, then drained

1 vegetable stock cube

4 garlic cloves, finely chopped

1 tsp maple syrup

1 tbsp red wine vinegar

juice of ½ lime

handful of fresh coriander

sea salt

I became obsessed with black beans on my travels around Latin America, and these Cuban black beans *(frijoles negros)* are tasty, versatile and batch-cooking friendly. Slowly cooking them from dried allows the flavours to intensify. This is a recipe you can leave to cook while you check off some items on your to-do list, so make a big batch and roll them out with the delicious serving options!

Serve them with fluffy **White Rice, Lime & Coriander [1]** – so simple. Alternatively, serve them in a vibrant **Tortilla Salad Bowl [2]** that includes crunchy salted tortilla chips, fresh lettuce, coriander, guac and beans, topped with a tasty Dijon dressing. Finally, transform these beans into a feast of **Cuban Black Bean Fajitas with Salsa & Guac [3]**. If you like, you can also add your favourite vegan faux meat substitute.

Heat the oil in a deep pan over a medium heat. Add the onion and green pepper and sauté for 4 minutes until softened, then add the cumin, paprika, oregano and tomato purée and continue to cook, stirring, for another 4 minutes. Add a splash of water if the onion starts to stick.

Add the bay leaves and black beans, then pour in enough water to cover and crumble in the stock cube. Season to taste with salt, then add the garlic and maple syrup. Bring to the boil, then reduce the heat, cover the pan and simmer for 30 minutes.

After 30 minutes, give it a stir and check to see if any more water is needed, adding a splash if necessary. Stir in the red wine vinegar then re-cover and continue to simmer, stirring occasionally, until the beans have softened, adding a splash of water if needed, which can take up to 2 hours. When ready, squeeze over the lime juice and sprinkle with fresh coriander.

The beans are now ready to be used in the recipes on pages 116–19, or will keep in the fridge for 3 days, or in the freezer for 3 months.

White Rice, Lime & Coriander

Option
One

Serves 2

~~~

200g (7oz) basmati rice, rinsed well under running water

2 servings of Cuban Black Beans (page 114)

sea salt

TO SERVE

1 lime, halved

handful of fresh coriander

1 tsp chilli flakes

Place the rice in a deep saucepan over a high heat and cover with 480ml (17fl oz) water. Season with salt and bring to the boil, then reduce the heat to low. Cover and leave to cook for 10 minutes, or until all the water has been absorbed. Remove from the heat and fluff up the rice with a fork.

Place the black beans in a saucepan over a medium heat and simmer for 6 minutes, until piping hot.

Serve the rice with the Cuban black beans, along with a squeeze of lime juice and a scattering of coriander and chilli flakes.

Cuban Black Bean Tortilla Salad Bowl

Serves 2

Option Two

2 servings of Cuban Black Beans (page 114)

100g (3½oz) salted tortilla chips

100g (3½oz) canned sweetcorn, drained

200g (7oz) mixed salad leaves

100g (3½oz) cherry tomatoes, quartered

1 chilli, sliced

2 spring onions, finely sliced

handful of fresh coriander

1 lime, halved

SIMPLE GUACAMOLE

2 avocados, peeled, stoned and sliced

1 tbsp lime juice

handful of fresh coriander, roughly chopped

sea salt and freshly ground black pepper

LEMON VINAIGRETTE

2 tbsp fresh lemon juice

1 tbsp white wine vinegar

1 tbsp maple syrup

3 tbsp extra-virgin olive oil

handful of fresh flat-leaf parsley, finely chopped

Place the black beans in a saucepan over a medium heat for 6 minutes until piping hot. Meanwhile, mash the avocados in a bowl, mix in the lime juice and coriander, and season with salt and pepper.

Now make the dressing: simply whisk all the ingredients for it in a small bowl or jug. Season with salt and pepper. Taste and adjust the sweet–sour balance if necessary.

Set out 2 salad bowls and arrange the tortilla chips around the sides of them (as shown on page 115). Add the sweetcorn and salad leaves. Top with the tomatoes, black beans, guacamole, chilli slices, spring onions, coriander and a squeeze of lime. Drizzle over the dressing and serve.

Cuban Black Bean Fajitas with Salsa & Guac

Option Three

Serves 2

1 tsp olive oil

1 red onion, sliced

1 red pepper, sliced

1 tsp fajita seasoning

100g (3½ oz) vegan chicken substitute (optional)

4 large soft tortilla wraps

2 servings of Cuban Black Beans (page 114)

1 Little Gem lettuce, sliced

2 tbsp hot sauce (optional)

handful of fresh coriander, roughly chopped

½ lime

sea salt

QUICK SALSA

2 large tomatoes, diced

¼ red onion, finely diced

1 tbsp fresh lime juice

1 tsp extra-virgin olive oil

handful of fresh coriander, roughly chopped

freshly ground black pepper

SIMPLE GUACAMOLE

2 avocados, peeled, stoned and sliced

1 tbsp lime juice

handful of fresh coriander, roughly chopped

Place the oil in a frying pan over a medium heat. When hot, add the onion and red pepper and cook for 5 minutes, then stir in the fajita seasoning and cook, stirring occasionally, for another 5 minutes. Mix in the vegan chicken (if using) and season to taste with salt.

Meanwhile, make the salsa: place all the ingredients for it in a bowl and mix together.

For the guacamole, mash the avocados in a bowl, then mix in the lime juice and coriander, and season with salt.

Place a second large frying pan over a medium heat and heat the wraps, one at a time, for 30 seconds on each side until hot and soft. Set aside on a plate and keep warm.

Meanwhile, place the black beans in a saucepan over a medium heat and simmer for 6 minutes, until piping hot.

Time to assemble your wraps! Lay out a warm wrap and start by adding a portion of black beans. Add some of the fajita-spiced onion mixture, then a layer of lettuce, followed by some guacamole, salsa and hot sauce (if using). Finish with a scattering of coriander and a squeeze of lime juice, and serve.

Braised Jerk Aubergine

Makes 4 servings

1 tbsp olive oil

4 aubergines, quartered lengthways and chopped into triangles

1 tbsp brown rice miso paste

2 tsp cornflour

1 spring onion, sliced

sea salt

SPICE PASTE

thumb-sized piece of fresh root ginger, grated

4 spring onions, roughly chopped

1 tbsp dried jerk seasoning

1 tsp allspice

½ tsp ground coriander

¼ tsp ground nutmeg

4 tbsp soy sauce

1½ tbsp maple syrup

2 tbsp red wine vinegar

2 tbsp olive oil

½ Scotch bonnet chilli, seeded (optional)

This one's for aubergine enthusiasts. First lightly char your aubergine, then cook in a slightly sweet and tangy jerk-spiced sauce.

Serve with **Rice & Peas & Plantain [1]**, my favourite way to eat anything jerk spice-based, and make sure to get that gravy into the rice and peas. Or combine the leftovers with pan-fried crispy paprika chickpeas to create my **Jerk Aubergine & Chickpea Quinoa Salad [2]**. For a quick, easy and satisfying meal, serve it alongside **Creamy Vegan Mac & Crisp Rocket [3]**.

Start by placing all the paste ingredients in a food processor and blending to form a coarse paste.

Place the oil in a large frying pan or wok over a medium heat until hot. Fry the aubergine chunks in batches for 2–3 minutes on each side until golden, sprinkling each batch with sea salt. Transfer to a plate and set aside.

Add the paste to the empty pan used for the aubergine and cook for 5 minutes, stirring occasionally. Now return the aubergine to the pan and stir to coat.

Add the miso paste and 240ml (8¼fl oz) water. Bring to the boil, then reduce the heat to medium for roughly 2 minutes. Put the cornflour in a small cup or bowl and mix with 2 teaspoons water to create a slurry. Add this to the pan and mix until the sauce thickens. Scatter over the chopped spring onion.

The jerk aubergine is now ready to be used in the recipes on pages 125–7, or it will keep in the fridge for 3 days, or in the freezer for 3 months.

Rice & Peas & Plantain

Option One

Serves 2

RICE & PEAS

2 portions of Braised Jerk Aubergine (page 122)

handful of fresh coriander

½ lime, halved

1 tbsp coconut oil

2 garlic cloves, minced

1 spring onion, finely sliced

240ml full-fat coconut milk

200g (7oz) basmati rice, rinsed under cold running water

½ x 400g (14oz) can kidney beans, drained

1 fresh thyme sprig

¼ Scotch bonnet chilli, seeded if you want less heat

sea salt and freshly ground black pepper

PLANTAIN

2 tbsp oil

1 plantain, peeled and cut into 2cm (1in) slices

Start by making the rice and peas: melt the coconut oil in a saucepan over a medium heat, then sauté the garlic and spring onion in it for 1 minute. Add the coconut milk, along with 240ml (8½fl oz) water, then mix in the rice and kidney beans. Season with salt and pepper, and add the thyme and chilli. Bring to the boil, then cover and reduce the heat to low. Cook for 10 minutes, until all the liquid has been absorbed. Fluff the rice with a fork and remove the chilli before serving.

For the plantain, heat the oil in a frying pan over a medium heat. Once hot, add the plantain slices in a single layer. Fry for 5 minutes until golden brown, then flip and fry on the other side. Remove from the pan and season with salt before serving.

Meanwhile, place the jerk aubergine in a deep pan over a medium heat for 7 minutes, stirring occasionally, until piping hot.

Serve in bowls alongside the rice and peas and plantain. Scatter over the fresh coriander and add a wedge of lime for squeezing over.

Jerk Aubergine & Chickpea Quinoa Salad

Option
Two

Serves 2

100g (3½oz) mixed quinoa, rinsed well under cold running water

2 tbsp olive oil

1 x 400g (14oz) can chickpeas, drained and rinsed

1 tbsp sweet smoked paprika

squeeze of fresh lime juice

handful of fresh flat-leaf parsley, finely chopped

2 portions of Braised Jerk Aubergine (page 122)

100g (3½oz) rocket

1 avocado, peeled, stoned and sliced

handful of curly leaf parsley, chopped

sea salt

COCONUT & LIME DRESSING

120g (4¼oz) unsweetened coconut yoghurt

1 tbsp olive oil

2 tbsp fresh lime juice

1 tsp maple syrup

handful of fresh coriander, finely chopped

Place the quinoa in a saucepan and cover with 200ml (7fl oz) water. Season with salt and bring to the boil, then reduce the heat to a simmer. Cover and cook for 10 minutes, until all the water has been absorbed. Fluff up with a fork before serving.

Meanwhile, heat the oil in a frying pan over a medium–high heat. Add the chickpeas and cook for 10 minutes, stirring occasionally, until golden. Stir in the paprika and season with a generous amount of salt. Turn off the heat and stir through the lime juice and parsley.

To make the dressing, place all the ingredients for it in a bowl and stir to combine. Season with salt.

To serve, place the quinoa, sautéed chickpeas, jerk aubergine, rocket, avocado and parsley in a large bowl and toss together. Drizzle over the coconut lime dressing or serve on the side.

Creamy Vegan Mac & Fresh Rocket

Option
Three

Serves 2

~~~

100g (3½oz) cashew nuts, soaked for at least 1 hour, then drained

¼ tsp garlic granules

¼ tsp ground turmeric

3 tbsp nutritional yeast

1 tbsp white miso paste

250g (9oz) dried macaroni

2 portions of Braised Jerk Aubergine (page 122)

sea salt and freshly ground black pepper

TO SERVE

2 spring onions, finely sliced

½ lemon, cut into wedges

handful of rocket

Place the cashew nuts in a blender, along with the garlic granules, turmeric, nutritional yeast and miso. Season with salt and pepper, add 240ml (8¼fl oz) water and blend until completely smooth.

Cook the pasta in a large pot of boiling salted water according to the packet instructions, until al dente. When ready, reserve a cupful of the cooking water, then drain the pasta in the usual way.

Return the pasta to the pan and place over a medium heat. Pour in the cashew nut sauce and stir to combine. Cook for 5 minutes until the sauce begins to thicken, then add a splash of the reserved pasta water and season with salt and pepper.

Meanwhile, place the jerk aubergine in a frying pan over a medium heat for 7 minutes, stirring occasionally, until piping hot. If the sauce starts to thicken, loosen with a splash of water.

Serve the vegan mac with the jerk aubergine, a sprinkling of spring onions, lemon wedges for squeezing over, and a side of fresh rocket.

One Tray

Chapter Three

Peri Peri Mushrooms

Makes 4 servings

500g (17½oz) oyster mushrooms

2 tbsp dry rub peri peri seasoning

2 tbsp coconut oil, melted

½ pineapple, peeled and chopped into chunks

sea salt

This is an incredibly simple way of adding spicy, tangy peri peri flavours to the tender, chewy and slightly crisp texture of oven-cooked oyster mushrooms. The recipe is really easy to put together and a favourite in my family. It makes a great base to turn into some weekday mealtime treats, or can even be the base of one big feast for friends and family.

Layer the oyster mushrooms and sweet warm pineapple with mayo, lettuce, avocado and hot sauce inside warm pitta breads to create **Peri Peri Pittas [1]**. This will give you all the flavours that I remember from trips to Nando's as a kid, Cook up some crispy **Potato Wedges & Slaw [2]** for a creamy, crunchy meal. Or remix it into a delicious salad by lightly charring sweetcorn to make flavourful **Peri Peri Charred Sweetcorn Salad Bowls [3]** with sundried tomatoes and creamy avocado tossed with fresh salad leaves and a vinaigrette dressing.

Preheat the oven to 240°C/220°C fan/475°F/gas 9.

Place the oyster mushrooms in a bowl, along with the peri peri seasoning, 1 tablespoon of the coconut oil and a generous pinch of salt. Mix to coat the mushrooms.

Brush a baking tray (or two, if needed) with the remaining oil and arrange the spice-coated mushrooms and pineapple chunks across the tray(s) in a single layer. Roast for 25 minutes, until brown and slightly crisp at the edges.

The mushrooms are now ready to be used in the recipes on pages 132–5, or will keep in the fridge for 3 days.

Peri Peri Pittas

Option One

Serves 2

2 portions of Peri Peri Mushrooms (page 130)

2 large pitta breads

1 avocado, peeled, stoned and sliced

½ red onion, finely sliced

handful of lettuce leaves

handful of fresh coriander

4 tbsp vegan mayonnaise

2 tbsp peri peri hot sauce (or other hot sauce)

lime wedges, for squeezing

Place a frying pan over a medium–high heat. When hot, add the peri peri mushrooms and warm through for 5 minutes, stirring occasionally, until piping hot.

Meanwhile, lightly toast the pitta breads in a toaster or under the grill.

Divide the hot mushrooms between the pitta breads, and add some of the avocado, red onion, lettuce and coriander. Finish each pitta with a drizzle of mayonnaise and hot sauce, and a squeeze of lime.

Potato Wedges & Slaw

Option Two

Serves 2

2 large Desiree potatoes, chopped into 1cm (½in) wedges or chips

2 tbsp olive oil

2 portions of Peri Peri Mushrooms (page 130)

handful of fresh coriander, roughly chopped

1 lime, cut into wedges

sea salt and freshly ground black pepper

SLAW

1 carrot, grated

¼ white cabbage, grated

3 tbsp vegan mayonnaise

Preheat the oven to 240°C/200°C fan/400°F/gas 9.

Bring a large pan of salted water to the boil. Add the potatoes and boil for 3 minutes, then drain.

Pour the olive oil into a roasting tray and place in the oven to heat for 1 minute. Remove and add the potatoes, coating them in the hot oil. Season with salt and roast for 25 minutes, turning once or twice, until golden brown and crisp.

Meanwhile, make the slaw. Place the grated carrot and cabbage in a large bowl. Add the vegan mayonnaise, season to taste with salt and pepper and mix well to create a creamy slaw.

Place a frying pan over a medium–high heat. When hot, add the peri peri mushrooms and warm through for 5 minutes, stirring occasionally, until piping hot.

Serve the mushrooms with the wedges, slaw, a sprinkle of fresh coriander and a lime wedge.

Peri Peri Charred Sweetcorn Salad Bowls

Option Three

Serves 2

2 corn on the cob

1 tbsp extra-virgin olive oil

handful of fresh coriander, roughly chopped

2 portions of Peri Peri Mushrooms (page 130)

200g (7oz) mixed salad leaves

120g (4¼oz) sundried tomatoes

1 avocado, peeled, stoned and sliced

DRESSING

2 tsp Dijon mustard

1 tbsp balsamic vinegar

6 tbsp extra-virgin olive oil

1 tbsp fresh lemon juice

sea salt and freshly ground black pepper

Lay one corn cob on a chopping board and carefully cut down the side of it with a sharp knife to remove the kernels. Rotate the cob so the cut side rests on the board and slice the kernels off another side. Continue rotating and slicing in this way until all the kernels have been removed.

To make the dressing, place all the ingredients for it in a bowl and mix to combine.

Place a frying pan over a medium heat. When hot, add the sweetcorn kernels. Cook for 5 minutes, until lightly charred. Turn off the heat and add the olive oil and coriander. Transfer to a large salad bowl, season with salt and mix well.

Return the empty frying pan to a medium–high heat. When hot, add the peri peri mushrooms and warm through for 5 minutes, stirring occasionally, until piping hot.

Add the salad leaves, tomatoes, avocado, charred sweetcorn and peri peri mushrooms to the salad bowl and mix well. Drizzle over the dressing just before serving.

Suya Grilled Vegetables

Main
Recipe

Makes 4 servings

1 large red onion, chopped into chunks

1 red pepper, chopped into chunks

1 green pepper, chopped into chunks

4 large portobello mushrooms, halved

200g (7oz) oyster mushrooms

2 tbsp olive oil

sea salt

SUYA SPICE MIX

80g (2¾oz) peanuts

4 tbsp ground ginger

2 tbsp smoked paprika

1 ½ tbsp garlic granules

½–1 tsp cayenne pepper

2 tsp salt

2 tbsp soy sauce

Suya spice rub is enjoyed across West Africa, where it is eaten on different meats that are grilled on skewers. It consists mainly of ground peanuts, which are infused with spices to give a warming heat to foods. In my vegan version, veggies are generously coated in a suya rub, threaded onto skewers and roasted in the oven, but they can also be charred on a barbecue to get an authentic taste of West African street food in a plant-based way.

First up, I suggest you create my **Suya Kebab Wraps [1]** by serving the charred veggies in soft flatbreads with tzatziki, chilli sauce and pickled cabbage for a burst of delicious flavours and textures. Remix the leftovers to build a fresh **Kale Salad with Peanut Vinaigrette [2]**, which includes juicy tomatoes and crunchy cucumber. I also love to serve the kebabs alongside fragrant and golden brown **Jollof with Plantain & Salad [3]**.

If using bamboo skewers, soak them in water 30 minutes before starting. Preheat the oven to 200°C/180°C fan/400°F/gas 6.

First make the spice mix: place the peanuts in a food processor and pulse until ground – be careful not to overmix, or they will turn into peanut butter. Transfer to a bowl and mix in the rest of the dry ingredients. Stir in the soy sauce and 4 tablespoons water. If the mixture feels too coarse and stiff, add a splash more water to loosen.

Place the onion, peppers and mushrooms in a large bowl. Pour over the suya spice mix and stir well to coat, then use your hands to rub the mixture into the vegetables.

Thread the vegetables onto skewers and place on a roasting tray or, if you prefer, simply spread out the veg in the tray. Drizzle with olive oil, sprinkle with sea salt, then roast in the oven for 25–30 minutes.

The grilled vegetables are now ready to be used in the recipes on pages 141–4, or will keep in the fridge for 3 days, or in the freezer for 3 months.

ONE TRAY

Suya Kebab Wraps

Option
One

Serves 2

~~~

2 portions of Suya Grilled Vegetables (page 138)

4 flatbreads

handful of lettuce

PICKLED CABBAGE

100g (3½oz) red cabbage, shredded

2 tbsp fresh lemon juice

½ tsp salt

CHILLI SAUCE

120g (4¼oz) red bird's-eye chillies, seeded

2 shallots

1 tbsp white vinegar

1 tbsp olive oil

1 tsp maple syrup (or other sweetener of your choice)

sea salt

TZATZIKI

120g (4¼oz) unsweetened coconut yoghurt

50g (1¾oz) cucumber, grated

1 tbsp olive oil

1 tbsp fresh lemon juice

handful of fresh dill, finely chopped

First make the pickled cabbage: simply mix all the ingredients for it together in a bowl and set aside.

For the chilli sauce, place the chillies and shallots in a blender and blitz to form a fine paste. Transfer to a saucepan and cook over a low heat for 5 minutes, until thickened. Remove from the heat and stir in the vinegar, olive oil and maple syrup or sweetener of your choice. Season with salt and set aside to cool (it is best served cold).

Place the suya vegetables in a saucepan over a medium–high heat and toss together for about 5 minutes until piping hot.

Meanwhile, place all the tzatziki ingredients in a bowl and mix well.

Heat the flatbreads in a dry frying pan over a medium heat for 1–2 minutes.

To serve, place each flatbread on a plate and top with the suya vegetables, tzatziki, chilli sauce, pickled cabbage and lettuce.

Kale Salad with Peanut Vinaigrette

Option
Two

Serves 2

~~~

100g (3½oz) kale, any woody stalks removed

juice of ½ lemon

2 tbsp extra-virgin olive oil

1 Romaine lettuce, roughly chopped

100g (3½oz) cherry tomatoes, halved

½ cucumber, sliced

1 red onion, finely sliced

2 portions of Suya Grilled Vegetables (page 138)

sea salt

PEANUT VINAIGRETTE

2 tbsp peanut oil

2 tbsp rice vinegar

1 tsp soy sauce

1 tbsp maple syrup

Place the kale in large bowl and add the lemon juice and oil. Season with salt, then use your hands to massage the oil and lemon juice into the kale for a few minutes. Add the lettuce, cherry tomatoes, cucumber and red onion and toss to combine.

Place the suya vegetables in a saucepan over a medium–high heat and toss together for about 5 minutes until piping hot.

Mix all the vinaigrette ingredients together in a small jug or bowl.

Serve the salad alongside the suya vegetables, with the peanut vinaigrette on the side for drizzling.

Jollof with Plantain & Salad

Serves 2

2 portions of Suya Grilled
Vegetables (page 138)

1 large tomato, sliced

handful of lettuce, shredded

lime wedges, to serve

JOLLOF

1 tbsp olive oil

1 small red onion, chopped

2 tbsp tomato purée

1 tsp curry powder

1 tsp ground ginger

1 bay leaf

1 large tomato, roughly chopped

2 garlic cloves, minced

1 red pepper, chopped

¼–½ Scotch bonnet chilli, seeded

200–300ml (7–10fl oz) vegetable
stock

200g (7oz) basmati rice, rinsed well
under cold running water

sea salt

PLANTAIN

1 tbsp oil

1 plantain, preferably yellow with
brown marks, peeled and sliced

To make the jollof, heat the oil in a deep saucepan over a medium heat. Add the red onion and sauté for 3 minutes until translucent, then add the tomato purée, curry powder, ginger and bay leaf. Season with salt and cook for 5 minutes, stirring occasionally. If the spices start to stick to the pan, add a splash of water or oil to loosen them.

Meanwhile, place the tomato, garlic, pepper and Scotch bonnet in a food processor and blend. Note the volume of the mixture and add the vegetable stock, a little at a time, until you have 460ml (16fl oz) of liquid.

Add this liquid to the pan, along with the rice. Season with salt once more and stir to combine. Bring to the boil, then reduce the heat to the lowest setting. Cover the pan and cook for 15 minutes. Remove from the heat, keeping the lid on, and let the steam continue to cook the rice for another 10 minutes, until all the liquid has been absorbed. Fluff up the rice before serving.

Meanwhile, make the plantain: heat the oil in a frying pan over a medium heat. Add the plantain slices in a single layer and cook for 5 minutes until golden brown, then turn to cook the other side. Sprinkle with sea salt before serving.

Place a frying pan on a medium heat, add the suya vegetables and cook for 6 minutes, stirring occasionally, until piping hot.

Serve the vegetables with the jollof, plantain, sliced tomatoes, lettuce and lime wedges.

Roasted Cauliflower Curry

Main
Recipe

Makes 4 servings

1 tbsp coconut oil

2 tsp garam masala

1 tsp ground turmeric

½ tsp ground coriander

2 tsp black mustard seeds

handful of curry leaves

1 tsp salt

400ml (14fl oz) can coconut milk

1 tsp mango chutney

thumb-sized piece of fresh root ginger, grated

1 red chilli, chopped

2 large tomatoes, chopped

1 large onion, chopped

1 red pepper, chopped

1 cauliflower, broken into florets

1 potato, peeled and chopped into 2cm (1in) chunks

1 x 400g (14oz) can chickpeas, drained and rinsed

fresh coriander, to serve

A mainstay weekday meal, hearty and flavourful, this is cooked in one big tray and roasted in the oven. Serve it with **Brown Rice, Mint Yoghurt & Cavolo Nero [1]** or **White Rice, Coconut Yoghurt, Coriander & Chutney [2]** for two quick and different weeknight dinners. Then turn the leftovers into a warming **Curried Cauliflower Salad with Turmeric & Tahini Dressing [3]**.

Preheat the oven to 160°C/140°C fan/320°F/gas 3.

Melt the coconut oil in a large, deep roasting tray over a medium heat. Add all the spices, along with the curry leaves and salt, and cook for 4 minutes, until fragrant and the mustard seeds start to pop slightly.

Add the rest of the ingredients, except the coriander, and mix well to combine. Cover with a lid or foil and transfer to the oven. Roast for 40 minutes, then remove the covering and roast for a further 15 minutes. Sprinkle with the fresh coriander before serving.

The curry is now ready to be used in the recipes on pages 148–50, or will keep in the fridge for 3 days, or in the freezer for 3 months.

Brown Rice,
Mint Yoghurt
& Cavolo Nero

Option
One

Serves 2

~~

200g (3½oz) brown rice, rinsed well under cold running water

2 portions of Roasted Cauliflower Curry (page 146)

100g (3½oz) cavolo nero (or you can use kale)

1 tbsp fresh lemon juice

sea salt

MINT YOGHURT

50g (1¾oz) unsweetened coconut yoghurt

1 tbsp fresh lemon juice

1 tsp extra-virgin olive oil

handful of fresh mint

handful of fresh coriander

Place the rice in a saucepan over a high heat and cover with 500ml (18fl oz) salted water. Bring to the boil, then reduce the heat, cover and leave to cook for 40 minutes, or until all the water has been absorbed.

Meanwhile, place the cauliflower curry in a saucepan over a medium heat and bring it to the boil. Reduce the heat to low and simmer for 6 minutes, until piping hot. Add a splash of water if the curry begins to look a bit dry.

To make the mint yoghurt, simply place all the ingredients for it in a bowl and mix together.

Place the cavolo nero in a frying pan over a medium heat, add a splash of water and sauté for 3 minutes until slightly wilted. Season with salt and squeeze over the lemon juice.

To serve, divide the curry and rice between two bowls with the cavolo nero and mint yoghurt on the side.

White Rice, Coconut Yoghurt, Coriander & Chutney

Option
Two

Serves 2

200g (7oz) basmati rice, rinsed well under cold running water

2 portions of Roasted Cauliflower Curry (page 146)

sea salt

TO SERVE

handful of fresh coriander

2 tbsp mango chutney

2 tbsp unsweetened coconut yoghurt

Place the rice in a deep saucepan over a high heat, and cover with 480ml (16fl oz) water. Season with salt and bring to the boil, then reduce the heat to low. Cover and leave to cook for 10 minutes, or until all the water has been absorbed. Remove from the heat and fluff up the rice with a fork.

Meanwhile, place the cauliflower curry in a saucepan over a medium heat and bring it to the boil. Reduce the heat to low and simmer for 6 minutes, until piping hot. Add a splash of water if the curry begins to look a bit dry.

To serve, divide the curry and the rice between two bowls. Scatter over the coriander and serve with a spoonful of mango chutney and coconut yoghurt.

Curried Cauliflower Salad with Turmeric & Tahini Dressing

Option
Three

Serves 2

200g (7oz) mixed greens (such as kale, spinach and lettuce leaves)

100g (3½oz) cherry tomatoes, halved

2 portions of Roasted Cauliflower Curry (page 146)

DRESSING

3 tbsp tahini

½ tsp ground turmeric

1 tbsp fresh lemon juice

1 tsp extra-virgin olive oil

1 tsp maple syrup

First make the dressing: simply place all the ingredients for it in a bowl and mix together. All tahinis vary in texture, so if the dressing seems too thick, add a splash of water to loosen it.

Place the mixed greens and cherry tomatoes in a large salad bowl and toss together, then top with the curried cauliflower. Dress with the tahini and turmeric dressing and serve.

Harissa Butter Bean Traybake

Main
Recipe

Makes 4 servings

3 tbsp rose harissa paste

1 tbsp maple syrup

1 tbsp olive oil

1 red pepper, chopped into chunks

4 carrots, chopped into 1cm (½in) slices on the diagonal

200g (7oz) mushrooms

2 red onions, quartered

4 garlic cloves, crushed

300g (10½oz) plum tomatoes, halved

1 x 400g (14oz) can butter beans, drained and rinsed

handful of fresh parsley

sea salt and freshly ground black pepper

Maximum flavour and minimal effort make this recipe a winner! Let the harissa paste do the talking in this super-simple yet extremely delicious traybake, your new go-to quick meal.

Serve it with a **Mint & Pomegranate Couscous [1]** plus a side of peppery rocket and a drizzle of green tahini for the ultimate flavour combo. Roll over the leftovers and eat alongside **Salad with Pitta & Hummus [2]** – you can also pop all the ingredients into the pitta to make sandwiches instead of serving it up in a bowl. Alternatively, enjoy this traybake with a delicious and vibrant **Wild Rice & Walnut Salad [3]**, which comes with tangy dried cranberries and a sweet mustard vinegar dressing.

Preheat the oven to 200°C/180°C fan/400°F/gas 6.

Put the harissa paste, maple syrup and olive oil into a small bowl and mix together.

Place the vegetables, garlic and tomatoes in a large, deep roasting tray. Drizzle the harissa mixture over the top and mix so that everything is well coated. Season with salt and pepper.

Put the tray in the oven for 20 minutes, then stir in the butter beans and return to the oven for another 20 minutes.

Scatter the fresh parsley over the vegetables just before serving.

The traybake is now ready to be used in the recipes on pages 154–7, or will keep in the fridge for 3 days, or in the freezer for up to 3 months.

Mint & Pomegranate Couscous

Option One

Serves 2

~

2 portions of Harissa Butter Bean Traybake (page 152)

100ml (3½fl oz) vegetable stock

100g (3½oz) couscous

handful of fresh mint

2 tbsp pomegranate seeds

1 tbsp fresh lemon juice

100g (3½oz) rocket

sea salt and freshly ground black pepper

Green Tahini Dressing (page 33), to serve

Preheat the oven to 200°C/180°C fan/400°F/gas 6.

Put the harissa butter bean traybake in a roasting tray and place in the oven for 6 minutes, or until piping hot. Take care not to overcook.

Meanwhile, place the vegetable stock in a saucepan and bring to the boil. Stir in the couscous, then cover and remove from the heat. Leave to steam for 5 minutes.

Fluff up the couscous with a fork, then stir in the mint, pomegranate seeds and lemon juice, and season with salt and pepper.

Serve the traybake with the couscous, offering the rocket on the side with a drizzle of the tahini dressing.

Salad with Pitta & Hummus

Option Two

Serves 2

~

2 portions of Harissa Butter Bean Traybake (page 152)

4 pitta breads

150g (5oz) mixed salad leaves

½ cucumber

100g (3½oz) cherry tomatoes, sliced

handful of fresh coriander

juice of ½ lemon

1 tbsp extra-virgin olive oil

4 tbsp hummus

sea salt and freshly ground black pepper

Preheat the oven to 200°C/180°C fan/400°F/gas 6.

Put the harissa butter bean traybake in a roasting tray and place in the oven for 6 minutes, or until piping hot. Take care not to overcook.

Lightly toast the pitta breads in a toaster or under the grill, then cut into strips.

Meanwhile in a large bowl, combine the mixed salad leaves, cucumber and cherry tomatoes. Scatter over the coriander, then drizzle with the lemon juice and olive oil and season with salt and pepper. Toss together, then serve on a plate with the traybake, the hot pittas and a side of hummus.

Wild Rice & Walnut Salad

Option
Three

Serves 2

~~~

2 portions of Harissa Butter Bean Traybake (page 152)

200g (3½oz) wild rice, rinsed well under cold running water

handful of walnuts, roughly chopped

2 tbsp dried cranberries

60g (2¼oz) wild rocket

handful of fresh flat-leaf parsley, roughly chopped

DRESSING

2 tbsp extra-virgin olive oil

2 tbsp white wine vinegar

1 tsp maple syrup

½ tsp Dijon mustard

Preheat the oven to 200°C/180°C fan/400°F/gas 6.

Put the harissa butter bean traybake in a roasting tray and place in the oven for 6 minutes, or until piping hot. Take care not to overcook.

Place all the dressing ingredients in a small jug or bowl, mix well, then set aside.

Place the rice in a deep saucepan over a high heat, and cover with 500ml (18fl oz) water. Season with salt and bring to the boil, then reduce the heat to low. Cover and leave to cook for 45 minutes, or until all the water has been absorbed. Remove from the heat and fluff up the rice with a fork.

Allow the rice to cool, then transfer to a salad bowl and add the walnuts, cranberries, rocket and parsley. Drizzle over the dressing and toss to combine, then serve alongside the traybake.

Roasted Red Peppers & Cherry Tomatoes

Main
Recipe

Makes 4 servings

4 red romano peppers, cut in half

110ml (4fl oz) olive oil

1 tbsp balsamic vinegar

4 garlic cloves, sliced

200g (7oz) cherry tomatoes, halved

2 tsp capers, drained

sea salt and freshly ground black pepper

BASIL DRESSING

60g (2¼oz) fresh basil leaves, finely chopped

1 garlic clove, minced

1 tbsp extra-virgin olive oil

2 tbsp fresh lemon juice

A versatile summertime dish of sweet red peppers roasted with juicy, slightly sour tomatoes, salty capers, garlic, olive oil and balsamic vinegar, then topped with a fresh basil dressing.

First up, you can serve it with **Garlicky Potatoes & Tahini Greens [1]** – the kale and long-stem broccoli work so well with the lemony tahini dressing. Transform the leftovers by simply blending the roasted red peppers and cherry tomatoes into a delicious sauce to create **Roasted Red Pepper & Cherry Tomato Pasta [2]**. Finally, you can add the juicy roast peppers and cherry tomatoes to a plate of tasty, slightly tangy **Courgette Cannellini Bean Salad [3]** tossed in lemon vinaigrette.

Preheat the oven to 200°C/180°C fan/400°F/gas 6.

Lay the pepper halves skin-side down in a shallow baking tray and drizzle over 2 tablespoons of the olive oil. Sprinkle with the balsamic vinegar and garlic slices, then season with salt and pepper. Roast for 20 minutes, then scatter the tomatoes and capers inside the peppers and roast for a further 5–10 minutes, until the peppers are tender and slightly charred. Set the tray aside to cool.

Meanwhile, make the dressing by combining all the ingredients and seasoning with salt and pepper. Drizzle the basil dressing over the peppers before serving.

These are now ready to be used in the recipes on pages 160–161, or will keep in the fridge for 3 days.

Garlicky Potatoes & Tahini Greens

Option One

Serves 2

200g (7oz) new potatoes
3 tbsp olive oil
2 garlic cloves, sliced
2 portions of Roasted Red Peppers & Cherry Tomatoes (page 158)
150g (5½oz) long-stem broccoli
200g (7oz) kale
handful of fresh parsley
sea salt and freshly ground black pepper

LEMON TAHINI DRESSING

2 garlic cloves, grated
2 tbsp fresh lemon juice
50g (1¾oz) tahini
½–1 tsp maple syrup

Preheat the oven to 200°C/180°C fan/400°F/gas 6. Cook the potatoes in a large pan of boiling salted water for 15 minutes until tender, then drain well.

Lightly oil a roasting tray and add the potatoes. Using a fork, flatten each potato but keep in one piece. Season with salt and pepper, sprinkle with the garlic and add a drizzle of olive oil. Roast until golden brown, adding the broccoli for the final 10 minutes and the kale for the final 5 minutes.

Meanwhile, combine all the dressing ingredients in a bowl and season to taste. If too thick, loosen with 1 tablespoon water.

Sprinkle the potatoes with sea salt, pepper and parsley. Serve on a plate with the red peppers and cherry tomatoes and your tahini greens.

Roasted Red Pepper & Cherry Tomato Pasta

Option Two

Serves 2

250g (9oz) pasta
2 portions of Roasted Red Peppers & Cherry Tomatoes (page 158)
handful of fresh parsley, chopped
2 tbsp nutritional yeast

Bring a large saucepan of lightly salted water to the boil, add the pasta and cook according to the packet instructions until al dente. Drain, reserving some of the cooking water.

Meanwhile, add the roasted peppers and tomatoes to a blender and blitz into a sauce. Pour into a saucepan and heat until hot – about 3 minutes. Add the cooked pasta and stir to combine, adding a splash of the reserved water to loosen it.

Serve the pasta in bowls, sprinkled with fresh parsley and nutritional yeast.

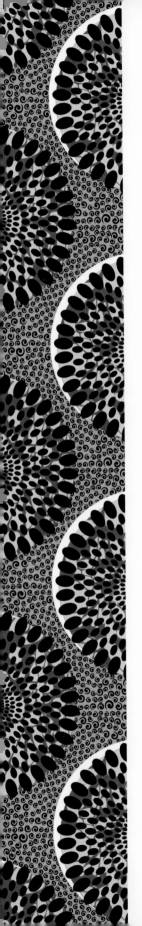

Courgette & Cannellini Bean Salad

Option Three

Serves 2

2 tbsp olive oil

1 courgette, cut into 1cm (½in) slices

1 x 400g (14oz) can cannellini beans, drained

¼ cucumber, diced

handful of fresh mint, chopped

handful of fresh coriander, chopped

2 portions of Roasted Red Peppers & Cherry Tomatoes (page 158)

sea salt and freshly ground black pepper

LEMON VINAIGRETTE

2 tbsp fresh lemon juice

1 tbsp white wine vinegar

1 tbsp maple syrup

3 tbsp extra-virgin olive oil

handful of fresh flat-leaf parsley, finely chopped

Heat the oil in a griddle pan over a medium heat until the pan is hot. Add the courgette slices and cook for 4 minutes until they are starting to turn brown and griddle marks appear. Turn over and cook on the other side for another 4 minutes until golden brown. Season with salt and black pepper.

For the lemon vinaigrette, place all the ingredients in a bowl and stir to combine.

In a bowl, toss the cannellini beans with the cucumbers, mint and coriander and a splash of the lemon vinaigrette.

Serve the roasted red peppers and tomatoes cold with the griddled courgettes, cannellini bean mix and its juices.

As someone who absolutely loves delicious food, I can honestly say I've never enjoyed food as much as I have on this plant-based journey.

Rachel Ama

Sticky Cauliflower Bites

Main
Recipe

Makes 4 servings

120g (1¾oz) plain flour

1 tbsp cornflour

120ml (4fl oz) plant-based milk

1 tsp garlic granules

80g (2¾oz) breadcrumbs

1 large cauliflower, broken into florets

2 tbsp sesame seeds

sea salt and freshly ground black pepper

STICKY SAUCE

2 garlic cloves, minced

1 tbsp grated fresh root ginger

3 tbsp soy sauce

2 tbsp maple syrup

1 tbsp white wine vinegar

1 tsp chilli flakes

1 tsp tomato purée

1 tsp cornflour

Not your average cauliflower recipe by any stretch of the imagination. This is battered, baked, then coated in a sticky, slightly spicy sauce and topped with sesame seeds. It's a crowd-pleaser, so serve it to friends or family and double up the sauce if you want it extra saucy.

Enjoy this simple dish with fluffy **White Rice & Sesame Seeds [1]** drizzled with a citrusy dressing. Use the leftovers to create a **Crunchy Sesame Salad [2]** – sliced raw veg in a tangy soy and ginger dressing. For something fun, roll into **Chinese-style Pancakes with Cucumber [3]** filled with crunchy peppers and spring onions and finished with a drizzle of hoisin sauce.

Preheat the oven to 240°C/220°C fan/475°F/gas 9 and line a deep roasting tray with baking paper.

Place the flours in a bowl, add the plant-based milk and garlic granules and whisk to create a batter. Season with salt and pepper. Spread out the breadcrumbs on a large plate. Dip a cauliflower floret in the batter, then roll it in the breadcrumbs and pop it into the prepared tray. Repeat with the remaining florets. Bake for 20 minutes, then transfer to a plate and set aside.

Place all the sauce ingredients, except the cornflour, in the roasting tray. Add 3–4 tablespoons water, stir to combine and place over a medium heat. Mix the cornflour and 1 tablespoon water in a small cup or bowl to make a slurry. Pour this into the sauce and keep stirring for a few minutes until it begins to thicken. Stir in the battered cauliflower until fully coated in the sauce. Sprinkle with the sesame seeds before serving.

The sticky cauliflower is now ready to be used in the recipes on pages 166–9, or it will keep in the fridge for 3 days.

White Rice
& Sesame Seeds

Option
One

Serves 2

200g (7oz) basmati rice, rinsed well under cold running water

2 portions of Sticky Cauliflower Bites (page 164)

TO SERVE

1 spring onion, finely sliced

handful of fresh coriander, chopped

1 tbsp sesame seeds

½ lime, cut into wedges

Preheat the oven to 220°C/200°C fan/425°F/gas 7. Line a deep roasting tray with baking paper.

Place the rice in a deep saucepan over a high heat and cover with 480ml (16fl oz) water. Season with salt and bring to the boil, then reduce the heat to low. Cover and leave to cook for 10 minutes, or until all the water has been absorbed. Remove from the heat and fluff up the rice with a fork.

Place the cauliflower bites in a roasting tray and reheat in the oven for 5 minutes until piping hot.

Serve the cauliflower bites with the rice, garnished with the spring onion, fresh coriander and sesame seeds, and with lime wedges for squeezing over.

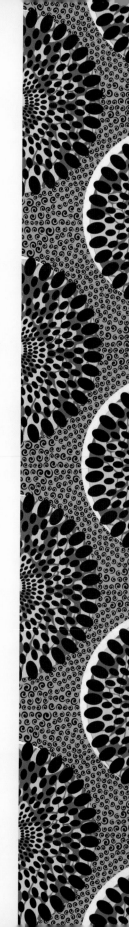

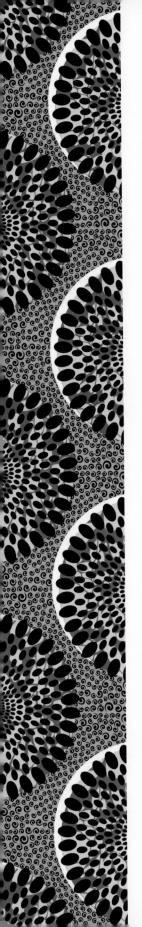

Crunchy Sesame Salad

Option
Two

Serves 2

1 tbsp coconut oil

100g (3½oz) long-stem broccoli, sliced lengthways

100g (3½oz) watercress

1 carrot, sliced into matchsticks

1 cucumber, sliced into matchsticks

2 portions of Sticky Cauliflower Bites (page 164)

handful of fresh coriander, chopped

handful of fresh mint, chopped

sea salt and freshly ground black pepper

SOY & GINGER DRESSING

2 tbsp rice vinegar

2 tbsp soy sauce

1 tbsp grated fresh root ginger

1 tbsp sesame oil

3 tbsp olive oil

1 tbsp maple syrup

Heat the oil in a saucepan over a medium heat. Add the broccoli, season with salt and pepper and cook for 5 minutes, tossing occasionally, until tender.

Meanwhile, make the dressing: put all the ingredients for it in a small bowl or jug and whisk together.

To assemble the salad, arrange the watercress, carrot and cucumber in 2 bowls, along with the broccoli and the cauliflower bites. Scatter over the coriander and mint and serve with the dressing on the side.

Chinese-style Pancakes with Cucumber

Option Three

Serves 2

~~

2 portions of Sticky Cauliflower Bites (page 164)

8 Chinese-style pancakes (or use soft tortillas instead)

¼ cucumber, sliced into fine matchsticks

2 spring onions, sliced into fine matchsticks

½ red pepper, sliced into fine matchsticks

60ml (4 tbsp) hoisin sauce

Preheat the oven to 220°C/200°C fan/425°F/gas 7.

Place the cauliflower bites in a roasting tray and reheat in the oven for 5 minutes until piping hot.

Meanwhile, steam the pancakes (or warm the tortillas) according to the packet instructions. Place them on a serving plate and cover to keep warm.

Arrange the cucumber, spring onions and red pepper on a plate or separate plates so that people can help themselves. Set out a bowl of hoisin sauce for dipping.

To assemble a pancake, place a few cauliflower bites in the middle and top with some of the cucumber, spring onion and red pepper. Roll up the pancake and dip in the hoisin sauce before eating.

Basics

Chapter Four

Cheeze Sauce

/ Main
Recipe

Makes 4 servings

250g (9oz) cashew nuts

4 tbsp nutritional yeast

1 tbsp white miso paste

1 tsp vegan Dijon mustard

½ tsp ground turmeric

1 tsp garlic granules

sea salt

A very easy and addictive recipe, this creamy vegan sauce is given an umami kick by white miso and nutritional yeast. It is extremely versatile, and should serve you well as a go-to recipe for all of your cheezy sauce needs.

For a quick and delicious **Mac & Cheeze [1]**, simply stir the sauce through macaroni pasta until lovely and thick. Also try adding a touch of nutmeg and layering it between pasta sheets with a rich tomato ragu for a **Vegetable Lasagne [2]** – it makes for a super creamy dish. Finally, add this cheeze sauce to a Mexican-inspired **Cheezy Crunch Wraps [3]**, which includes fresh tomatoes and lettuce, jalapeño-infused black beans and crunchy tortilla chips all wrapped up in a large tortilla and toasted like a quesadilla.

Place all the ingredients in a high-speed blender. Add 440ml (15fl oz) water and blend until completely smooth. You should end up with about 600ml (20fl oz) of sauce.

The sauce is now ready to be used in the recipes on pages 174–6, or it will keep in the fridge for 3 days, or in the freezer for 3 months.

Easy Vegan
Mac & Cheeze

Option
One

Serves 2

250g (9oz) macaroni pasta

2 portions (300ml/10fl oz) of
Cheeze Sauce (page 172)

sea salt and freshly ground black
pepper

Cook the pasta in a large pot of boiling salted water according to the packet instructions until al dente. When ready, reserve a cupful of the cooking water, then drain the pasta as usual.

Return the pasta to the pan and place over a medium heat. Stir in the cheeze sauce and heat until the sauce begins to thicken. Add a splash of the reserved water if the sauce has thickened too much and season with salt and pepper. Serve immediately.

Vegetable Lasagne

Option
Two

Serves 2

~~~

1 tbsp olive oil

½ courgette, chopped into 1cm
(½in) sliced into circles

½ red onion, finely chopped

½ celery stick, finely chopped

1 small carrot, finely chopped

½ aubergine, chopped into 1cm
(½in) cubes

2 garlic cloves, minced

1 tsp tomato purée

½ tsp dried oregano

400g (14oz) passata

½ tbsp brown rice miso paste

200g (7oz) canned lentils or
vegan mince

200ml (7fl oz) vegetable stock

handful of fresh flat-leaf parsley,
chopped

sea salt

2 portions (300ml/10fl oz) of
Cheeze Sauce (page 172)

½ tsp ground nutmeg

4 dried lasagne sheets

Preheat the oven to 200°C/180°C fan/400°F/gas 6.

Heat the oil in a deep frying pan over a medium heat and add the courgette pieces in a single layer. Season with salt and cook for 2–3 minutes until lightly browned. Turn the pieces over and cook for a further few minutes until lightly browned. Transfer to a plate and set aside for now.

Place the onion, celery and carrot in the empty pan and cook for 7 minutes, stirring occasionally, until the vegetables begin to soften. Add the aubergine, garlic, tomato purée and oregano, and cook for a further 2 minutes. Add the passata, miso paste, lentils and vegetable stock. Bring to the boil, then cover with a lid, reduce the heat to low and simmer for 15 minutes, stirring occasionally. When the time is up, remove the lid and cook for another 5 minutes so that the sauce thickens and the carrot softens.

Set out a small baking dish. Spread a layer of the tomato mixture in the bottom. Top this with a layer of cooked courgettes, followed by a layer of cheeze sauce. Sprinkle with nutmeg, then cover with the lasagne sheets. Add the remaining tomato mixture, followed by the remaining courgettes, then top with the remaining cheeze sauce and sprinkle with a little more nutmeg.

Bake for 40 minutes, or according to the instructions on the lasagne packet. Remove from the oven and rest for 5 minutes before serving.

Cheezy Crunch Wraps

Serves 2

~~

4 tsp olive oil

½ red onion

½ tsp paprika

½ tsp dried oregano

½ tsp ground coriander

1 tsp ground cumin

2 garlic cloves, crushed

1 tbsp chopped jalapeño chillies

200g (7oz) canned black beans, drained and rinsed

2 large soft flour tortillas and 2 small soft flour tortillas

2 portions (300ml/10fl oz) of Cheeze Sauce (page 172)

2 small taco shells, roughly broken, or a handful of lightly salted tortilla chips

80g (2¾oz) Romaine lettuce, shredded

sea salt and freshly ground black pepper

TOMATO SALSA

2 large tomatoes, finely chopped

handful of fresh coriander

1 tbsp fresh lime juice

Heat 3 teaspoons of the oil in a deep saucepan over a medium heat. Add the onion, paprika, oregano, ground coriander and cumin, and cook for 3 minutes, until the onion starts to soften. Stir in the garlic, jalapeños and black beans, along with 80ml (2¾fl oz) water. Cook for another 5 minutes, then use a potato masher or fork to mash some of the beans. Continue to cook for a further 5 minutes until all the liquid has been absorbed.

Meanwhile, make the salsa. Place the chopped tomatoes, fresh coriander and lime juice in a bowl and stir to combine. Season with salt and pepper.

Pour the cheeze sauce into a small saucepan over a medium heat and warm for 5 minutes, stirring occasionally. It should start to thicken slightly.

To build your first wrap, lay out a large flour tortilla and place a scoop of the black bean mixture in the centre. Drizzle a generous amount of the thick cheeze sauce over the beans. Top with broken taco pieces or some tortilla chips, followed by some tomato salsa and lettuce. Place one of the small flour tortillas on top, then tightly fold up the edges of the large tortilla.

Heat the remaining teaspoon of olive oil in a large frying pan over a high heat. Add the wrap, upside down to keep it closed, and cook for 3 minutes until golden. Turn it over and cook for another 3 minutes until golden. Keep warm while you fill and cook the second wrap in the same way.

Walnut & Cauliflower Mince

Main
Recipe

Makes 4 servings

300g (10½oz) cauliflower florets

200g (7oz) walnuts

40g (1½oz) dried shiitake mushrooms

2 tbsp soy sauce

A tasty mixture of walnuts, cauliflower and mushrooms, this is an amazing alternative for faux vegan meat, The soy sauce and dried shiitakes add an extra depth of flavour, while the walnuts add not only texture and taste, but a high level of health-giving omegas.

Add the walnut and cauliflower mince to a rich tomato sauce with a pinch of cinnamon for my vegan take on Greek **Moussaka [1]**, a dish of layered potato, aubergine and creamy béchamel sauce made with plant-based milk. Turn the mince leftovers into a vegan **Spaghetti Bolognese [2]**, an everyday crowd-pleaser, or transform the mince into a flavourful and filling **Sweet Potato Shepherd's Pie [3]** layered with soft, sweet mash.

Preheat oven to 180°C/160°C fan/350°F/gas 4.

Place the cauliflower florets in a high-speed blender and pulse until they resemble rice. Transfer to a bowl. Now place the walnuts in the blender and pulse until they break down into little pieces, taking care not to overblend and end up with walnut butter. Add the walnuts to the bowl of cauliflower. Finally, place the shiitake mushrooms in the blender and blitz to form a powder. Add this to the walnuts and cauliflower, then add the soy sauce and mix well.

Transfer the mixture to a roasting tray and spread it out in an even layer. Place in the oven for 30 minutes, giving the mixture a good shuffle every 10 minutes to ensure the walnuts don't burn.

The mince is now ready to be used in the recipes on pages 180–2, or it will keep in the fridge for 3 days, or in the freezer for up to 3 months.

Walnut & Cauliflower Moussaka

Option One

Serves 2

~~~

2 tbsp olive oil

1 aubergine, sliced into 5mm (¼in) rounds

½ red onion, finely chopped

2 garlic cloves, finely chopped

½ tsp dried oregano

1 tsp tomato purée

1 bay leaf

1 tsp ground cinnamon

100ml (3½fl oz) red wine

2 portions of Walnut & Cauliflower Mince (page 178)

1 x 400g (14oz) can chopped tomatoes

200ml (7fl oz) vegetable stock

1 potato, peeled and cut into 5mm (¼in) rounds

BÉCHAMEL SAUCE

20g (¾oz) vegan butter

20g (¾oz) plain flour

230ml (7¾fl oz) plant-based milk, such as oat milk

½ tsp ground nutmeg

sea salt and freshly ground black pepper

Preheat the oven to 220°C/200°C fan/425°F/gas 7.

Heat 1 tablespoon of the olive oil in a frying pan over a high heat. Add the aubergine and fry for 6 minutes on each side until golden and beginning to soften. Transfer to a plate and set aside for now.

In the same pan, heat the remaining tablespoon of olive oil over a medium heat. Add the onion and cook for 5 minutes until browned and slightly caramelized, then add the garlic, dried oregano, tomato purée, bay leaf and cinnamon. Stir well to combine, then pour in the red wine. Bring to the boil and cook for 1–2 minutes, or until the wine is reduced by half. Now stir in the walnut and cauliflower mince, along with the chopped tomatoes and vegetable stock. Bring back to the boil, then reduce the heat to low and simmer, covered, for 15 minutes.

Meanwhile, bring a large pan of lightly salted water to the boil. Add the potato slices and cook for 5 minutes, then drain. Allow the potato slices to steam dry for 10 minutes.

To make the béchamel sauce, melt the butter in a small saucepan over a medium heat. Stir in the flour and cook for about 1 minute. Remove from the heat and whisk in a splash of plant-based milk. Keep adding it in small splashes, whisking until smooth. Return the pan to the heat and whisk for a minute, then season with nutmeg, salt and pepper. The sauce should be smooth and thick.

To assemble the moussaka, spoon half the walnut mixture into a small ovenproof dish and spread it out evenly. Cover with a layer of cooked potato, then a layer of aubergine. Repeat these layers once more, then top with the béchamel sauce, spreading it smoothly.

Bake for 30 minutes, then set aside to cool for 10 minutes before serving.

Walnut & Cauliflower Spaghetti Bolognese

Option
Two

Serves 2

1 tbsp olive oil

½ red onion, finely chopped

½ celery stick, finely chopped

1 carrot, finely chopped

2 garlic cloves, finely chopped

1 tsp tomato purée

1 bay leaf

100ml (3½fl oz) red wine

2 portions of Walnut & Cauliflower Mince (page 178)

1 x 400g (14oz) can chopped tomatoes

240ml (8¼fl oz) vegetable stock

1 tsp brown rice miso paste

250g (9oz) spaghetti

handful of fresh flat-leaf parsley

sea salt and freshly ground black pepper

TO SERVE

Handful of fresh parsley, chopped

2 tbsp nutritional yeast (optional)

1 tbsp extra-virgin olive oil for serving

Heat the oil in a large pan over a medium heat. Add the onion, celery and carrot, and cook for 5 minutes until the onion is browned and slightly caramelized. Stire in the garlic, tomato purée and bay leaf, then pour in the red wine. Bring to the boil and cook for about 5 minutes until the wine is reduced by half.

Now add the walnut and cauliflower mince, along with the chopped tomatoes and vegetable stock. Bring back to the boil, then cover and reduce the heat to low. Simmer for 30 minutes until the carrot has completely softened. Remove the lid and stir, then cook for a further 5 minutes to allow the sauce to thicken slightly.

Meanwhile, cook the spaghetti in a large saucepan of salted boiling water according to the packet instructions until al dente. When ready, reserve a cupful of the cooking water, then drain the spaghetti and return it to the pan.

Add the sauce to the spaghetti and stir together over a low heat. Add a splash of the reserved pasta water and cook for 2 minutes until completely combined.

Serve immediately in bowls, sprinkled with fresh parsley and nutritional yeast (if using), and a drizzle of extra-virgin olive oil.

Sweet Potato Shepherd's Pie

Serves 2

~

1 tbsp olive oil

½ onion, finely chopped

½ leek, finely chopped

1 carrot, finely chopped

2 garlic cloves, finely chopped

1 tsp tomato purée

2 fresh thyme sprigs

1 bay leaf

100ml (3½fl oz) red wine

2 portions of Walnut & Cauliflower Mince (page 178)

1 x 400g (14oz) can chopped tomatoes

240ml (8¼fl oz) vegetable stock

1 tsp vegan Worcestershire sauce or Marmite

1 potato, peeled and chopped

1 sweet potato, peeled and chopped

1 tbsp vegan butter

2 tbsp nutritional yeast (optional)

1 tbsp extra-virgin olive oil

handful of fresh flat-leaf parsley, chopped

sea salt and freshly ground black pepper

Heat the olive oil in a large pan over a medium heat. Add the onion, leek and carrot and cook for 5 minutes until the onion has browned. Add the garlic, tomato purée, thyme sprigs and bay leaf. Stir to combine, then pour in the red wine. Bring to the boil and cook for about 5 minutes until the wine has reduced by half.

Now add the walnut and cauliflower mixture, along with the chopped tomatoes, vegetable stock and Worcestershire sauce. Bring to the boil, then cover and reduce the heat to low. Simmer for 15 minutes. Remove the lid and stir, then cook for a further 5 minutes to allow the sauce to thicken slightly.

Meanwhile, cook the potato and sweet potato in a large pan of boiling salted water for 15 minutes until soft. Drain, then return to the pan. Add the vegan butter and nutritional yeast (if using). Season with salt and pepper and mash until smooth.

To assemble the shepherd's pie, spoon the walnut and cauliflower mixture into a small baking dish. Top with the mashed potatoes and spread evenly, then use a fork to roughen up the surface. Drizzle with the extra-virgin olive oil and bake for 30 minutes until the top has browned.

Allow to cool for 5 minutes before serving sprinkled with the fresh parsley.

Slow-roast Tomatoes

Main
Recipe

Makes 4 servings

450g (1lb) large tomatoes, halved

300g (10½oz) medium-sized
tomatoes, halved

250g (9oz) cherry tomatoes, halved

1 garlic bulb, cloves separated
and peeled

3 tbsp olive oil

1 tbsp balsamic vinegar

sea salt and freshly ground black
pepper

Lightly drizzled with olive oil, balsamic vinegar and a sprinkling
of salt, these tomatoes, slowly roasted with garlic, slightly
caramelize, which deepens and intensifies their natural flavour.
For the best result, be sure to make them in peak tomato season.

For a speedy meal, create **Slow-roast Tomato Bruschette
[1]**, with a creamy cashew and chive spread, topped with
fresh basil and flaky salt. Another option is to transform these
jammy tomatoes into **Slow-roast Tomato Pasta with Lemon
Breadcrumbs [2]** for a comforting weeknight dinner. The
lemon and garlic breadcrumbs are a crunchy contrast to the soft
pasta. Refresh any leftover slow-roasted tomatoes on top of a
Roast Fennel & Cannellini Bean Salad [3] tossed in a lemon
vinaigrette.

Preheat the oven to 160°C/140°C fan/320°F/gas 3.

Arrange all the tomatoes and the garlic in a large roasting tray.
Drizzle with the olive oil and balsamic vinegar, and loosely mix to
coat. Season with salt and pepper and roast for 60 minutes.

The slow-roast tomatoes are now ready to be used in the recipes on
pages 186–9, or will keep in the fridge for 3 days, or in the freezer for
up to 3 months.

Slow-roast Tomato Bruschette

Option One

Serves 2

2 portions of Slow-roast Tomatoes (page 184)

1 medium ciabatta, cut into 2cm (¾in) slices

Handful of fresh basil

1 tbsp extra-virgin olive oil

flaky sea salt

CASHEW CREAM

130g cashews, soaked in water for at least 1 hour

1 tbsp lemon juice

1 tbsp nutritional yeast

sea salt and freshly ground black pepper

few chives, chopped

Preheat the oven to 190°C/170°C fan/375°F/gas 5.

To make the cashew cream, drain the cashew nuts and place in a blender with the lemon juice, nutritional yeast and a sprinkling of salt and pepper. Blend until smooth, using a spatula to push down the spread now and then. If it is stuck or too thick, add a small splash of water to loosen it, but not too much, as we want to keep it thick. Transfer to a bowl and mix in the chopped chives.

Toast the ciabatta in the oven for a few minutes until hot and lightly browned on both sides.

Spread the toast with the cashew cream, then top with the slow-roast tomatoes and fresh basil. Add a sprinkling of flaky sea salt, some black pepper and a drizzle of olive oil to each slice and serve straight away.

Slow-roast Tomato Pasta with Lemon Breadcrumbs

Option
Two

Serves 2

250g (9oz) pasta

1 tsp olive oil

1 tsp fresh lemon juice and a grating of zest

1½ tbsp panko breadcrumbs

2 portions of Slow-roast Tomatoes (page 184)

1 tbsp nutritional yeast

handful of fresh basil

sea salt and freshly ground black pepper

Cook the pasta in a large saucepan of boiling salted water according to the packet instructions until al dente. When ready, reserve a cupful of the cooking water, then drain the pasta and set aside.

Heat the oil in a non-stick frying pan over a medium heat. Add the lemon juice and zest, then toss in the breadcrumbs and toast them for a few minutes, stirring often, until golden. Season with salt, then quickly transfer the crumbs to a cold bowl and mix in the nutritional yeast.

Place the slow-roast tomatoes in large saucepan over a high heat. Add the cooked pasta and stir together, then reduce the heat to medium. As it warms, pour in a little of the pasta water to loosen. Continue to cook, stirring, until everything is piping hot and the pasta is beginning to take on the colour of the tomatoes.

Serve sprinkled with fresh basil, the lemon breadcrumbs and black pepper.

Roast Fennel & Cannellini Bean Salad

Option
Three

Serves 2

~

2 fennel bulbs, sliced into 2cm
(1in) wedges

1 x 400g (14oz) can cannellini
beans, drained and rinsed

1 tbsp olive oil

1 tbsp fresh lemon juice

2 fresh thyme sprigs, leaves picked

2 garlic cloves, sliced

2 portions of Slow Roast Tomatoes
(page 184)

200g (7oz) mixed salad leaves

sea salt and freshly ground black
pepper

LEMON VINAIGRETTE

2 tbsp fresh lemon juice

1 tbsp white wine vinegar

1 tbsp maple syrup

3 tbsp extra-virgin olive oil

handful of fresh flat-leaf parsley,
finely chopped

Preheat the oven to 220°C/200°C fan/425°F/gas 7.

Arrange the fennel wedges in a large roasting tray. Add the cannellini beans and drizzle over the olive oil and lemon juice. Scatter over the thyme leaves and garlic, then season with salt and pepper. Give everything a good stir to combine.

Roast for 20 minutes, then remove from the oven and roughly mix. Return to the oven and roast for another 10 minutes, until the fennel has slightly caramelized.

Meanwhile, whisk all the dressing ingredients together in a small bowl or jug. Season with salt and pepper. Taste and adjust the sweet–sour balance as necessary.

Transfer the roasted fennel and cannellini beans to a large serving dish. Add the mixed salad leaves and slow-roast tomatoes. Drizzle over the dressing and serve.

Puff Pastry

Makes 1 sheet

120g (4½oz) cold vegan block of
butter, plus 1 tbsp extra
for crumbling

240g (8½oz) plain flour, plus extra
for dusting

1 tsp salt

160ml (5½fl oz) cold water

A sheet of light, multi-layered puff pastry is really useful for making a range of dishes, both sweet and savoury. As a vegan, buying pastries is something I had to let go of for the longest time, but this recipe has saved me from that pastry fomo. If you're short on time, you can use store-bought puff pastry for the options, but this recipe is a winner!

For a big dessert for friends and family (or maybe just yourself!) create a show-stopping **Plum & Peach Galette [1]**. What could be nicer than warm plums and peaches on buttery pastry with a spoonful of vanilla ice cream? Alternatively, cut the pastry into squares and top each one with your favourite vegan melty cheese, a large slice of tomato and fresh basil and pop them in the oven for delicious, savoury **Tomato & Cheeze Pastries [2]**. Finally, you can never go wrong with **Apple Tarts [3]**, one of my favourite treats. They go down perfectly with a cup of tea.

Grate the block of vegan butter into a bowl or onto a plate and place in the freezer while you continue with the recipe.

Place the flour and salt in a large bowl and combine with a fork. Crumble the extra 1 tablespoon of vegan butter into the flour until it resembles breadcrumbs. Gradually stir in the cold water, mixing together with your hand to form a dough. Keep bringing the dough together until you can clean the sides of the bowl with it. Dust a clean surface with flour and knead the dough for about 2 minutes until you have a smooth, soft ball. Place it in an airtight container in the fridge for 30 minutes so that the vegan butter solidifies.

Lightly flour a clean surface, then roll the chilled dough into a rectangle roughly 5mm (¼in) thick. Remove the frozen butter from the freezer and sprinkle roughly two-thirds of it across the lower two-thirds of the rectangle. Fold the top third of dough into the middle of the buttered area and use a pastry brush to dust off any flour still sticking to it, then fold the remaining buttered dough over it so you have a thick, triple-decker rectangle. Turn the pastry through 90 degrees, then roll it into a rectangle roughly 5mm (¼in) thick and repeat the previous steps with the remaining frozen butter. Remember always to dust off any extra flour that may stick from the work surface as you go.

After the final rolling, fold the pastry into thirds and press the edges together. Place in an airtight container in the fridge for at least 1 hour. When the time is up, lightly flour a clean surface and roll the chilled pastry into a rectangle again. Fold into thirds as before, dusting off any excess flour as you go. Seal the ends and place in the fridge for 30 minutes. The pastry is now ready to use in the recipes on pages 192–195.

Plum & Peach Galette

Option One

Serves 4

2 tbsp maple syrup

1 tbsp fresh lime juice + 1 tsp lime zest and extra to serve

1 tsp vanilla extract

pinch of salt

400g (14oz) plums, stoned and cut into ½cm (¼in) slices

400g (14oz) peaches, stoned and cut into ½cm (¼in) slices

2 tsp cornflour

1 sheet of Puff Pastry (page 190)

plain flour, for dusting

4 scoops of plant-based vanilla ice cream, to serve

Preheat the oven to 200°C/180°C fan/400°F/gas 6.

Place the maple syrup in a large bowl and stir in the lime juice and zest, vanilla and salt. Add the plums and peaches and toss them gently to coat. Evenly sprinkle them with the cornflour and again gently toss together.

Lightly flour a clean surface and roll the pastry into a circle about 30cm (12in) in diameter. Use the rolling pin to transfer it to a non-stick baking sheet. Place the fruit in the centre of it, leaving a 2.5cm (1in) border all around the edge. Fold up this border, pinching it together at intervals, so it encloses the fruit.

Place in the oven and bake for 30 minutes, until golden.

Serve the galette with the ice cream and a sprinkling of lime zest.

Tomato & Cheeze Pastries

Option
Two

Makes 4

∿

1 sheet of Puff Pastry (page 190)

flour, for dusting

12 slices of vegan cheese

2 large tomatoes, sliced

fresh basil leaves

1 tbsp extra-virgin olive oil

sea salt and freshly ground black pepper

Preheat the oven to 200°C/180°C fan/400°F/gas 6.

Place the pastry on a lightly floured surface and roll it into a 38 x 25cm (15 x 10in) rectangle. Cut it into 6 equal pieces – typically 13cm (5in) square but they can vary slightly.

Place 2 slices of vegan cheese in opposite corners of each pastry square. Sit a tomato slice on each slice of cheese. Add a basil leaf or two, season with salt and pepper, then fold the empty corners into the middle to meet in the centre of the pastry.

Place the pastries on a large baking sheet and bake for 20 minutes they are until golden and the cheese has melted. Drizzle with the olive oil before serving.

Apple Tarts

Option
Three

Makes 4

~~~

1 sheet of Puff Pastry (page 190)
flour, for dusting
6 tbsp unsweetened apple sauce
3 apples, cored and thinly sliced
3 tbsp maple syrup (or other liquid sweetener of choice)
2 tbsp icing sugar (optional)

Preheat the oven to 200°C/180°C fan/400°F/gas 6.

Place the pastry on a lightly floured surface and roll it into a 38 x 25cm (15 x 10in) rectangle. Cut it into 6 equal pieces – typically 13cm (5in) square but they can vary slightly.

Put 1 tablespoon of apple sauce in the centre of each square, then top with overlapping slices of the apple. Bake for 20 minutes until golden.

Remove from the oven and brush with maple syrup or your preferred sweetener to give the tarts a gloss. Dust with icing sugar, if you like.

Roast Vegetables

Makes 4 servings

1 courgette, chopped into 2.5cm (1in) half-moons

2 carrots, chopped into 1cm (½in) slices

1 beetroot, peeled and chopped into 1cm (½in) chunks

1–2 tbsp olive oil

1 red pepper, chopped into 2.5cm (1in) chunks

1 yellow pepper, chopped into 2.5cm (1in) chunks

1 garlic bulb, cloves separated and peeled

1 red onion, cut into quarters

1 tsp dried oregano

1 tsp dried parsley

200g (7oz) cherry tomatoes, halved

1 large head of broccoli, broken into florets

sea salt and freshly ground black pepper

When I am short of time for cooking prep, my favourite thing is to roast vegetables. Drizzled with a touch of olive oil, seasoned with parsley and oregano, they are tasty and super-versatile for making a variety of other dishes. They are also really good to make when I need to clear old produce from the fridge.

You can enjoy these vegetables with brown rice, creamy avocado and fresh herbs to make a colourful and nourishing **Brown Rice Rainbow Veg Bowl [1]** that's both simple and satisfying. Or refresh the roast vegetables to create a **Vegan Sausage & Vegetable Traybake [2]**, which is topped with watercress sprigs and a generous drizzle of basil dressing. Combine the rest of the veg into a delicious **Roasted Veg Salad & Beetroot Hummus [3]** and serve with fresh warm pittas.

Preheat the oven to 220°C/200°C fan/425°F/gas 7.

Place the courgette, carrots and beetroot in a large roasting tray. Drizzle with 1 tablespoon olive oil and roast for 20 minutes.

Add the peppers, garlic and red onion, then scatter over the dried oregano and parsley. Season with salt and pepper, then toss everything together to coat the vegetables in the herbs and oil.

Roast for a further 20 minutes, then remove from the oven and toss again. Add the tomatoes and broccoli to the tray, along with the remaining 1 tablespoon olive oil (if needed). Return to the oven and roast for another for another 15 minutes, until all the vegetables are golden and cooked through.

The roast veg are now ready to be used in the recipes on pages 198–201, or will keep in the fridge for 3 days, or in the freezer for up to 3 months.

Brown Rice Rainbow Veg Bowl

Option One

Serves 2

~~~

200g (7oz) brown rice, rinsed well under cold running water
2 portions of Roast Vegetables (page 196)
1 avocado peeled, stoned and chopped
handful of fresh parsley, roughly chopped
sea salt

MAPLE MUSTARD DRESSING

2 tsp Dijon mustard
1 tbsp balsamic vinegar
6 tbsp extra-virgin olive oil
1 tbsp lemon juice
1 tbsp maple syrup

Preheat the oven to 220°C/200°C fan/425°F/gas 7.

Place the rice in a deep saucepan over a high heat and cover with 500ml (18fl oz) water. Season with salt and bring to the boil, then reduce the heat to low, cover with a lid and cook for 45 minutes, or until all the water has been absorbed. Remove from the heat and fluff the rice with a fork.

While the rice is cooking, place all the dressing ingredients in a bowl and whisk together until smooth.

Reheat your roast vegetables by spreading them over a roasting tray and placing in the oven for 4–5 minutes until hot.

Serve the roast vegetables and brown rice with the chopped avocado, a large handful of fresh parsley and a drizzle of the dressing.

Vegan Sausage & Vegetable Traybake

Option Two

Serves 2

〜〜〜

4 vegan sausages

2 portions of Roast Vegetables (page 196)

60g (2¼oz) watercress

BASIL DRESSING

60g (2¼oz) fresh basil leaves, finely chopped

1 garlic clove, minced

1 tbsp extra-virgin olive oil

2 tbsp fresh lemon juice

sea salt and freshly ground black pepper

Preheat the oven to 200°C/180°C fan/400°F/gas 6.

Place the sausages in a roasting tray and place in the oven for 10 minutes. Add the roast vegetables to the tray and return to the oven for another 10 minutes, until the sausages are cooked through and the vegetables are piping hot.

Meanwhile, place all the dressing ingredients in a small bowl or jug and whisk to combine.

Arrange the sausages and roast vegetables on 2 plates along with the watercress. Drizzle over the basil dressing and serve.

Roasted Veg Salad & Beetroot Hummus

Option
Three

Serves 2

2 portions of Roast Vegetables
(page 196)

100g (3½oz) mixed salad leaves

1 avocado, peeled, stoned and sliced

2 pitta breads, toasted

SPICED BEETROOT HUMMUS

250g (9oz) beetroot, chopped into
2.5cm (1in) chunks

1 tsp olive oil

1 x 400g (14oz) can chickpeas,
drained

1 tbsp bicarbonate of soda
(optional)

2 garlic cloves, minced

juice of ½ lemon

1 tsp tahini

½ tsp ground coriander

½ tsp ground cumin

¼ tsp ground cinnamon

sea salt and freshly ground black
pepper

MAPLE MUSTARD DRESSING

2 tsp vegan Dijon mustard

1 tbsp balsamic vinegar

6 tbsp extra-virgin olive oil

1 tbsp fresh lemon juice

1 tbsp maple syrup

Preheat the oven to 200°C/180°C fan/400°F/gas 6.

To prepare the hummus, place the beetroot in a shallow, ovenproof baking dish. Drizzle over the olive oil to lightly coat, then cover with a lid and roast for 50–60 minutes until tender. Set aside to cool.

For super-smooth hummus, follow this optional extra step. Place the chickpeas in a small saucepan over a low heat. Add the bicarbonate of soda and stir for 1 minute, then pour over enough water to cover the chickpeas. Cook on the same low heat for about 5 minutes until the skins begin to fall off. Drain and transfer the chickpeas to a large bowl. Place the bowl under cold running water and rub the chickpeas between your hands to help loosen their skins further. Using a sieve or your hands, scoop out and discard the skins floating on the surface. This can take 3 changes of water. You don't have to remove them all, but the more you remove, the smoother the hummus will be.

Place the garlic, lemon juice, tahini and spices in a bowl and mix to form a paste. Season to taste with salt and pepper. If the mixture seems too thick, add a little water to loosen it. Do this 1 tablespoon at a time until you reach the consistency you want.

Place the chickpeas and roasted beetroot in a food processor and blend into a coarse paste. Then, with the processor still running, pour in the tahini mixture and blend until fully combined.

Now make the dressing by mixing all the ingredients for it in a small bowl or jug and mix well. Season with salt and pepper.

Reheat your roasted vegetables by spreading them over a roasting tray and place in the oven for 4–5 minutes until hot.

Combine the roast vegetables, salad leaves and avocado in a large bowl. Pour over the dressing and toss to coat. Serve alongside the spiced beetroot hummus, with toasted pitta breads on the side.

Stir-fried Vegetables

Makes 4 servings

1 tbsp coconut oil

4 garlic cloves

1 red chilli, finely chopped

1 courgette, sliced into 2.5cm (1in) half-moons

2 red peppers, sliced

3 spring onions, finely chopped

2 carrots, finely sliced

1 tbsp capers, finely chopped

200g (7oz) broccoli, roughly chopped

sea salt and freshly ground black pepper

Stir-frying vegetables is one of the quickest ways to make dinner, and one of the easiest ways to use up leftover odds and ends of vegetables from the fridge. Stir-fry these essentials and see how many delicious meals you can make.

Turn these veggies into a delicious sweet-savoury-sour **Quinoa Pad Thai [1]** for extra nutrients and a pack of protein. The tangy sauce instantly takes your veggies from basic to flavourful, so no surprise this is one of my favourite Thai dishes. For another take, stir-fry the veggies in a creamy, lightly spicy peanut sauce and add some noodles for the ultimate simple weekday meal – **Peanut & Vegetable Noodles [2]**. You can also refresh the veggies in a super-tasty **Vegetable Fried Rice [3]**, which is inspired by my time in Indonesia. Throw the veggies into a wok with cooked rice and toss in a tasty umami-packed sauce, then serve with a side of fresh sliced tomatoes and cucumbers.

Heat the coconut oil in a large wok over a high heat. Add all the ingredients and stir-fry, tossing frequently, for 4–5 minutes until all the vegetables are piping hot. Season with salt and pepper.

The stir-fried vegetables are now ready to be used in the recipes on pages 204–5, or will keep in the fridge for 3 days.

Quinoa Pad Thai

Option One

Serves 2

60g (2¼oz) mixed quinoa, rinsed well under cold running water

250g (9oz) rice noodles

1 tablespoon coconut oil

2 portions of Stir-fried Vegetables (page 202)

200g (7oz) beansprouts

1 tbsp peanut oil

sea salt

SAUCE

1 tsp tamarind paste

2 tbsp soy sauce

1 tbsp maple syrup

1 tbsp rice vinegar

TO SERVE

fresh coriander

1 tbsp chilli flakes

2 tbsp peanuts, crushed

lime wedges

Place the quinoa in a saucepan and cover with 120ml (4fl oz) water. Season with salt and bring to the boil, then reduce the heat and cover. Cook for 10 minutes until the water has been absorbed. Fluff up with a fork.

Meanwhile, cook the rice noodles according to the packet instructions, then drain. While the noodles are cooking, place all the sauce ingredients in a bowl, mix well, then set aside.

Heat the coconut oil in a wok or frying pan over a high heat. Add the stir-fried vegetables, noodles and quinoa, along with half the beansprouts, and cover with the sauce. Cook, stirring well, for 3 minutes until the sauce has been absorbed.

Divide the pad Thai between 2 plates or bowls and top with the remaining beansprouts. Drizzle over the peanut oil, sprinkle with the coriander, chilli flakes and crushed peanuts, and serve with lime wedges for squeezing over.

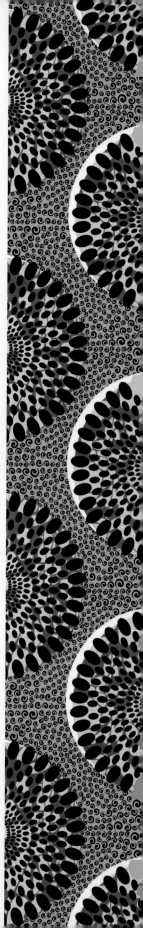

Peanut & Vegetable Noodles

Option Two

Serves 2

250g (9oz) wheat noodles

1 tbsp coconut oil

2 portions of Stir-fried Vegetables (page 202)

1 tbsp peanut oil

1 spring onion, sliced

fresh coriander

1 tbsp chilli flakes

lime wedges, to serve

SAUCE

2 tbsp smooth peanut butter with no added sugar

2 tbsp soy sauce

1 tbsp rice vinegar

1 tbsp maple syrup

Cook the noodles according to the packet instructions, then drain.

Meanwhile, mix together all the sauce ingredients in a bowl and set aside.

Heat the cocnut oil in a wok or frying pan over a high heat. Add the stir-fried vegetables and noodles. Pour over the sauce, mix together and cook, stirring, for 3 minutes.

Divide between 2 bowls or plates. Drizzle over the peanut oil, sprinkle with the spring onion, coriander and chilli flakes, and serve with lime wedges for squeezing over.

Vegetable Fried Rice

Option Three

Serves 2

200g (7oz) basmati rice, rinsed well

1 tbsp coconut oil

2 portions of Stir-fried Vegetables (page 202)

2 plum tomatoes, sliced

¼ cucumber, sliced

1 tsp chilli flakes

handful of fresh coriander

sea salt

lime wedges, to serve

SAUCE

1 tsp maple syrup (or sweetener of your choice)

1 tsp soy sauce

1 tsp tomato purée

1 tsp rice vinegar

1 chilli, seeded and finely chopped

Place the rice in a deep saucepan over a high heat and cover with 390ml (13¾fl oz) water. Season with salt and bring to the boil, then reduce the heat to low. Cover and cook for 10 minutes, or until all the water has been absorbed. Remove from the heat and fluff up the rice with a fork.

Meanwhile, combine all the sauce ingredients in a small jug or bowl and mix well.

Heat the coconut oil in a wok or large frying pan over a high heat. Add the stir-fried vegetables and cook for 2 minutes, then stir in the sauce and the cooked rice. Cook, stirring well to combine, until piping hot.

Serve with the tomatoes and cucumber, sprinkled with chilli flakes and fresh coriander, and lime wedges on the side for squeezing over.

Sushi Tray

Main Recipe

Makes 4 servings

400g (14oz) sushi rice, rinsed in cold running water

1 tbsp rice vinegar

2 carrots, sliced into ribbons

1 cucumber, sliced

2 spring onions, sliced

2 red peppers, sliced

4 nori sheets

2 limes, cut into wedges

MARINADE

3 tbsp rice vinegar

2 tbsp sugar

Prepare simple raw vegetables and freshly cooked sushi rice for a few days of delicious, easy eating – perfect for the warmer months.

Transform these carrots, peppers, spring onions into **Vegan Sushi Rolls [1]** with fresh avocado slices, pickled ginger and soy sauce for dipping. Use the leftovers to make big **Vegan Sushi Bowls [2]** containing edamame, sweet mango chunks and radish, with a soy ginger dressing on the side. Or you can transform them into **Rainbow Summer Rolls with Peanut Dressing [3]**, which are inspired by delicious Vietnamese Gỏi cuốn, otherwise known as fresh spring rolls made from rice paper filled with herbs and dipped into a peanut sauce.

Place the rice in a saucepan with 300ml (10fl oz) of cold water. Leave to soak for 30 minutes.

When the time is up, place the saucepan over a high heat and bring to the boil, then cover with a lid, reduce the heat to low and simmer for 10 minutes, or until the water has been absorbed. Set aside, still covered, for 10 minutes, then transfer the rice to a bowl and stir in 1 tablespoon of the rice vinegar.

For the sushi marinade, put the 3 tablespoons rice vinegar in a non-stick saucepan over a medium heat, add the sugar and stir until dissolved. Then, bit by bit, pour this mixture into the sushi rice bowl, mixing and fluffing to combine with the rice.

Place the bowl of prepared sushi rice on a tray. Arrange the rest of the ingredients in separate bowls and place on the tray too.

The sushi tray is now ready to be used in the recipes on pages 208–11, or it will keep in the fridge for 3 days.

Vegan Sushi Rolls

Option One

Serves 2

~

2 portions of Sushi Tray (page 206)

1 avocado, peeled, stoned and sliced

60ml (4 tbsp) soy sauce

2 tbsp pickled ginger

2 tbsp wasabi (optional)

PICKLE MIXTURE

3 tbsp rice vinegar

1 tbsp sugar

To make the pickle mixture, mix the vinegar and sugar in a bowl with 1 tablespoon water. Add the carrot ribbons from the sushi tray and rub the pickling mixture into them. Set aside for at least 15 minutes.

Lay one of the nori sheets from the sushi tray on a bamboo rolling mat or clean tea towel. Spoon some rice on top, then wet the spoon and use it to spread the rice towards the edges of the nori sheet, leaving a 1cm (½in) border all around.

Arrange the pickled carrot and avocado, along with some of the pepper, cucumber and spring onion from the tray, in a line down one side of the nori sheet.

Lightly dampen the edges of the sheet, then roll it up as tightly and neatly as possible, using the mat or tea towel to help you. Dip a sharp knife in water and use it to cut the roll into 4cm (1 ½in) pieces. Repeat with the remaining nori sheet and ingredients.

Serve the sushi rolls with the soy sauce for dipping, and offer the pickled ginger and wasabi (if using) on the side.

Vegan Sushi Bowls

Option Two

Serves 2

~

2 portions of Sushi Tray (page 206)

2 radishes, finely sliced

2 tsp black sesame seeds

200g (7oz) edamame beans, podded

1 mango, peeled, stoned and cut into chunks

SOY GINGER DRESSING

2 tbsp rice vinegar

2 tbsp soy sauce

1 tbsp grated fresh root ginger

1 tbsp sesame oil

3 tbsp olive oil

1 tbsp maple syrup

First make the dressing: put all the ingredients for it in a small bowl or jug and whisk together.

Arrange all the other ingredients in 2 large dishes to create beautiful rainbow sushi bowls, topped with sliced nori sheets from the sushi tray. Drizzle the dressing on top and serve.

Rainbow Summer Rolls with Peanut Dressing

Option
Three

Serves 2

6 sheets of rice paper

2 portions of Sushi Tray (page 206)

handful of fresh coriander, roughly chopped

handful of fresh mint, roughly chopped

¼ small red cabbage, finely sliced

6 Baby Gem lettuces

PEANUT DRESSING

3 tbsp smooth peanut butter

1 tbsp rice vinegar

1 tbsp soy sauce

1 tbsp maple syrup

First make the dressing: place all the ingredients for it in a small jug or bowl with 1 tablespoon water and whisk to combine. Add another tablespoon water if needed to create a smooth consistency.

Fill a bowl with warm water and place a sheet of rice paper in it to soak, turning occasionally. You want it to be pliable, but not limp. Do this one sheet at a time.

Cut the nori sheets from the sushi tray into thin slices (1cm/½in or less) as long as the rice paper diameter.

Arrange all the ingredients across the centre of a softened rice paper sheet in this order: rice, carrots, cucumber, spring onion, peppers, red cabbage, nori strips and a lettuce leaf.

Roll up like a burrito, folding in the short ends first, then rolling it up along the width. Place seam-side down on a serving plate. Repeat the filling and rolling process with the remaining rice paper sheets and ingredients. Serve with a bowl of the dressing for dipping.

Loaf
Cake Mix

Makes enough for 1 cake

300g (10½oz) plain flour

2 tsp baking powder

180g (6½oz) golden caster sugar

If you follow me on Instagram, you will be aware that I am a self-confessed cake lover, so I couldn't write a new book and not share my favourite cakes to make right now, even if they don't strictly fit the *One Pot Three Ways* style... Think of this as a fail-safe vegan cake recipe to have up your sleeve for when you want to whip up a tasty cake with ease. There is a misconception that vegan cakes are always dense, stale-tasting and horrible, but that's definitely not true in this case. Please let me show you how to make deliciously moist vegan cakes!

First up, use the basic mixture to make a **Lime & Ginger Loaf Cake with Coconut Whip [1]**. This is a summer recipe and, wow, I quickly became obsessed with it. Tangy limes and spiced ginger in a sweet and soft cake – my happy place. As basic as it may sound, I have always loved fresh oranges, especially when they are in season. I ate a lot of them when I was pregnant, so the soft **Orange Loaf Cake [2]** is for my fellow orange enthusiasts. And finally, be sure to try my **Marble Banana Bread [3]**, which is soft and tasty, with hints of chocolate – perfect with a nice cup of tea!

Sift the flour and baking powder into a large bowl. Stir to combine, then add the golden caster sugar. Mix well to ensure the various elements are evenly distributed.

The basic dry mixture is now ready to be used in the recipes on pages 214–16, or it will keep in a sterilized jar in the cupboard for up to a year.

Lime & Ginger Loaf Cake with Coconut Whip

Option One

Makes 1 cake

120ml (4fl oz) rapeseed oil, plus extra for greasing

1 full quantity of Loaf Cake Mix (page 212)

200ml (7fl oz) unsweetened plant-based milk of your choice

80ml (2¾fl oz) lime juice

20g (¾oz) fresh ginger

COCONUT WHIP

1 x 400g (14 oz) can full-fat coconut milk, placed upside down in the fridge overnight or for at least 2 hours (see Tip)

2 tbsp icing sugar

GLAZE

1 tbsp fresh lime juice

1 tsp finely chopped preserved stem ginger

1 tsp maple syrup

TO DECORATE

freshly grated lime zest

1 tbsp coconut flakes (optional)

Preheat the oven to 200°C/180°C fan/400°F/gas 6. Oil a 900g (2lb) loaf tin and line with baking paper.

Place the dry cake mix in a large bowl. In a separate bowl, mix together the rapeseed oil, plant-based milk, lime juice and ginger. Once well combined, pour this into the dry cake mix and beat together. Pour the batter into the prepared loaf tin and bake for 40–50 minutes. To check if it's done, insert a knife into the centre of the cake: if it comes out clean, your cake is ready; if not, return it to the oven for a few more minutes.

Let the cake cool in the tin for 10 minutes, then turn it onto a wire rack and leave to cool completely.

To make the coconut whip, open the chilled coconut milk and pour the separated water at the top into a container and reserve for other uses (such as smoothies, curries or juices). Add the thick coconut milk to a bowl and sift in the icing sugar. Whip with a hand-held electric whisk for at least 3 minutes until thick and creamy.

Now combine the glaze ingredients in a bowl and mix well. Drizzle this over the cake, then top with the whipped coconut cream. Finally, sprinkle with the lime zest and coconut flakes if using.

Store the cake in an airtight container at room temperature and eat within 3 days to enjoy at its best.

/ This recipe works best with full-fat coconut milk that doesn't contain any extra thickening agents, so check the ingredients on the label. Chilling the tin separates the water, which can be easily poured away to leave you with thick coconut cream, perfect for whipping. Note that some stores also sell coconut cream labelled specifically for whipping.

Orange Loaf Cake

Option Two

Makes 1 cake

120ml (4fl oz) rapeseed oil

1 full quantity of Loaf Cake Mix (page 212)

½ tsp bicarbonate of soda

200ml (7fl oz) unsweetened plant-based milk

130ml (4½fl oz) fresh orange juice

zest of 1 orange

1 tsp white vinegar

TOPPING

4 tsp fresh orange juice

1 tbsp maple syrup

4 tbsp icing sugar

4 orange slices

zest of ½ orange

Preheat the oven to 200°C/180°C fan/400°F/gas 6. Oil a 900g (2lb) loaf tin and line with baking paper.

Place the dry cake mix in a large bowl and mix in the bicarbonate of soda. In a separate bowl, mix together the rapeseed oil, plant-based milk, orange juice, orange zest and vinegar. Once well combined, pour this into the dry cake mix and beat together. Pour the batter into the prepared loaf tin and bake for 40–50 minutes. To check if it's done, insert a knife into the centre of the cake: if it comes out clean, your cake is ready; if not, return it to the oven for a few more minutes.

Let the cake cool in the tin for 10 minutes, then turn onto a wire rack and leave to cool completely.

For the topping, mix 3 teaspoons of the orange juice with the maple syrup and brush this over the cake like a glaze. Then mix together the icing sugar with the remaining teaspoon of orange juice and drizzle this mixture over the cake. Finally, arrange the orange slices on top and scatter over the orange zest.

Store the cake in an airtight container at room temperature and eat within 3 days to enjoy at its best.

Marble Banana Bread

Option Three

Makes 1 loaf cake

120ml (4fl oz) rapeseed oil, plus extra for greasing

1 full quantity Loaf Cake Mix (page 212)

½ tsp bicarbonate of soda

200ml (7fl oz) unsweetened plant-based milk of your choice

3 ripe bananas, mashed

1 tsp white vinegar

2 tbsp cocoa powder

/ If you want an extra chocolate kick, feel free to add some chocolate chips.

Preheat the oven to 200°C/180°C fan/400°F/gas 6. Oil a 900g (2lb) loaf tin and line with baking paper.

Place the dry cake mix in a large bowl and mix in the bicarbonate of soda. In a separate bowl, mix together the rapeseed oil, plant-based milk, mashed bananas and vinegar. Once well combined, pour into the dry cake mix and beat together.

Transfer half the batter to the bowl just used for mixing the wet ingredients (there's no need to rinse it). Add the cocoa powder and stir to combine.

Spoon dollops of each batter into the prepared loaf tin, alternating them so that the two colours are well distributed. Bake for 40–50 minutes. To check if the cake is done, insert a knife into the centre: if it comes out clean, your cake is ready; if not, return it to the oven for a few more minutes.

Let the cake cool in the tin for 10 minutes, then transfer to a wire rack and leave to cool completely.

Store the cake in an airtight container at room temperature and eat within 3 days to enjoy at its best.

Index

Acknowledgements

I have to start by thanking my mum. Wow, there are no words to summarise the last year. Throughout my life I've always felt your support and love. Watching you be the badass, resilient, strong, caring entrepreneurial super woman, super mum and super human that you are has both shaped me and continued to inspire me everyday. And this last year, just when I didn't think I could thank you enough, you stood by me through my pregnancy, my home birth — essentially you were my very own doula, supporting me becoming a mother myself whilst writing a book and working, and in a pandemic all the while having your own battles too, just wow. Mum. Thank you. Thank you over and over and over, you are my rock, my everyday inspiration and my best friend.

Remi, I wrote about how much you inspire me in my first book, look at you now, your first feature film, BIFA awarded and BAFTA! Now an uncle too to my lil man. Thank you for being you and always inspiring me.

My gu, it's been an incredibly hard year for you, had things been different I know you would have been by my side throughout. Thank you for the long phone calls and always being a big warm hug filled with love. Congratulations on being a great grandma, how lucky am I that my son gets to feel your love and know his welsh roots.

To my son's father, you've seen me write two books now, hope your 'prada' me. Thank you for believing in me as a mother, best friend and the work I put into creating this book.

To ish, it's been almost 15 years of friendship, I'd have lost the plot by now without you lol! Thank you for always, always being there for me.

A big thank you to Dad, James, Jos and my friends and family for being part of this journey, love always.

A big, big thank you to my management team, Alice, Daisy and T! So much love to each of you. For all the emails and phone calls, iMessages and WhatsApps making sure I'm meeting deadlines and always checking in that I am good and supported in these crazy times.

Thank you Jay, my Sierra Leone brother, from shooting my maternity pictures to the cover of this book and of course a few bits with my lil man. Your work is incredible, I'm so honoured to be able to work with you.

My publishing team at Yellow Kite, it has truly been amazing to see the vision of my book come to life with you all. Thank you for believing in this and my recipes as much as I do!

Nikki and Emma, I can't express how happy I am with the design of this book! Thank you so much for your dedication to capturing my voice through this book visually. You both really hit the nail on the head on what I had envisioned, it's beautiful, Thank you!

To Liz and Max, always an absolute pleasure working with you both, couldn't imagine doing a book without you two behind the lens. Thank you Ellie for helping to bring my recipes to life with styling even with nursery rhymes and baby music in the back. Thank you Louie for the amazing props.

First published in Great Britain in 2021 by Yellow Kite
An imprint of Hodder & Stoughton
An Hachette UK company

1

A CIP catalogue record for this title is available from
the British Library.

Hardback ISBN 978 1 529 36994 6
eBook ISBN 978 1 529 36995 3

Executive Publisher: Liz Gough
Project Editor: Isabel Gonzalez-Prendergast
Editorial Assistant: Olivia Nightingall
Copyeditor: Tara O'Sullivan
Art Direction: Nikki Dupin, Studio Nic & Lou
Design & Art Direction: Emma Wells, Studio Nic & Lou
Food Photography: Liz and Max Haarala Hamilton
Portrait Photography: Henry Jay Kamara
Food Stylist: Eleanor Mulligan
Props Stylist: Louie Waller
Senior Production Controller: Diana Talyanina

Colour origination by Alta London
Printed and bound in Germany by Firmengruppe APPL

Hodder & Stoughton policy is to use papers that are
natural, renewable and recyclable products and made
from wood grown in sustainable forests. The logging and
manufacturing processes are expected to conform to the
environmental regulations of the country of origin.

Yellow Kite
Hodder & Stoughton Ltd
Carmelite House
50 Victoria Embankment
London EC4Y 0DZ

www.yellowkitebooks.co.uk
www.hodder.co.uk